This book is about making choices – looking at situations and deciding what to do. We are constantly challenged to make decisions – to select from a variety of options.

Not only in business and professional situations do we face choices but also in everyday life. Fortunately, most of them are simple, routine, and safe. But life is filled with complicated, expensive, and sometimes dangerous situations – and that can make for difficult choices.

But consider this. No matter how complicated, confusing, or detailed a situation or a problem is, it eventually boils down to a simple "Yes – No" choice.

Just think about that for a moment. Ultimately, every decision we make has only two possibilities: yes – no, stay – go, add – subtract, up – down, etc.

The essays contained herein revolve around such options.

As you read them, consider what else could have been done, what you might have done or avoided doing, and what consequences could have developed.

Each essay is a "quick read," but hopefully you'll find yourself spending time considering the choices and the implications.

Enjoy the read.

We are constantly challenged to make decisions: looking at situations and selecting choices from a variety of options. Not only in business and professional situations are we faced with choices, but also in everyday life. Fortunately, most of them are simple, routine, and safe. However, life can be filled with complicated, expensive, and sometimes dangerous situations – and that can make for difficult decisions. J. Robert Parkinson PhD shows you how to sort through your options to make the best decisions available, boiling it down to a simple "yes/no" choice—information that can change your life!

KUDOS for *The Lowly Turtle*

In *The Lowly Turtle* by J. Robert Parkinson, PhD, there is a wealth of information and advice on communication, business skills, and decision making. A collection of motivational and informational essays, the book is well organized, well thought out, and well written. Covering everything from communication skills, managing techniques, and selling skills to technology and generational differences, the book is an excellent source of advice and inspiration. I especially like the way Parkinson presents his information in the form of easy-to-read-and-understand essays and teaches you how to apply the information to both your personal and professional life. ~ *Taylor Jones, The Review Team of Taylor Jones & Regan Murphy*

The Lowly Turtle by Dr. J. Robert Parkinson is another jewel in this talented and savvy businessman and author's string of self-help books. Focusing on the decisions-making process this time, Parkinson takes us through the mechanics of decision making and how the process relates to other skills we need to have, such as communication skills, selling skills, etc., skills that are essential for success in any aspect of life. But mostly the book is about how our everyday, seemingly small, decisions can have big consequences in our lives if we aren't paying attention. A natural teacher, Dr. Parkinson gets right to the heart of the matter, presenting his ideas and information in easy-to-read essays that get his points across without preaching, making it much more likely that we will take his message to heart and apply the principles he teaches. Well done. ~ *Regan Murphy, The Review Team of Taylor Jones & Regan Murphy*

ACKNOWLEDGMENTS

I want to thank the many people who have contributed the ideas, questions, and suggestions that formed this book. There are too many to name individually, but you know who you are. Some are close friends, some are distant acquaintances, and some are total strangers.

But I appreciate everything you offered. Thanks.

A special "Thank You" to Faith, who edited this book through numerous "Bumps in her road," and to Jack who created the artwork. I appreciate everything you did to make this an interesting professional work.

THE LOWLY TURTLE

J. ROBERT PARKINSON, PHD

A Black Opal Books Publication

GENRE: NON-FICTION/SELF-HELP

This book is a work of non-fiction. All information and opinions expressed herein are the views of the author. This publication is intended to provide accurate and authoritative information concerning the subject matter covered and is for informational purposes only. Neither the author nor the publisher is attempting to provide legal advice of any kind. All trademarks, service marks, registered trademarks, and registered service marks are the property of their respective owners and if used herein are for identification purposes only. The publisher does not have any control over or assume any responsibility for author or third-party websites or their contents.

THE LOWLY TURTLE
Copyright © 2017 by j Robert Parkinson, PhD
Cover Design by J. Robert Parkinson, PhD
All cover art copyright © 2017
All Rights Reserved
Print ISBN: 978-1-626946-59-0

First Publication: JUNE 2017

All rights reserved under the International and Pan-American Copyright Conventions. No part of this book may be reproduced or transmitted in any form or by any means, electronic or mechanical, including photocopying, recording, or by any information storage and retrieval system, without permission in writing from the publisher.

WARNING: The unauthorized reproduction or distribution of this copyrighted work is illegal. Criminal copyright infringement, including infringement without monetary gain, is investigated by the FBI and is punishable by up to 5 years in federal prison and a fine of $250,000. Anyone pirating our ebooks will be prosecuted to the fullest extent of the law and may be liable for each individual download resulting therefrom.

ABOUT THE PRINT VERSION: If you purchased a print version of this book without a cover, you should be aware that the book is stolen property. It was reported as "unsold and destroyed" to the publisher, and neither the author nor the publisher has received any payment for this "stripped book."

IF YOU FIND AN EBOOK OR PRINT VERSION OF THIS BOOK BEING SOLD OR SHARED ILLEGALLY, PLEASE REPORT IT TO: lpn@blackopalbooks.com

Published by Black Opal Books **http://www.blackopalbooks.com**

DEDICATION

To my wife, Eileen,

my first editor, and

my greatest supporter.

Nothing leaves the office without her okay.

This book is as much hers as it is mine.

TABLE OF CONTENTS

INTRODUCTION	1
CHAPTER 1: *Communication Skills*	6
CHAPTER 2: *Managing Techniques*	46
CHAPTER 3: *Customer Service*	86
CHAPTER 4: *Selling Skills*	120
CHAPTER 5: *Interviewing*	133
CHAPTER 6: *Technology*	147
CHAPTER 7: *Laughable Language*	167
CHAPTER 8: *Message Clarity*	191
CHAPTER 9: *Generational Differences*	210
CHAPTER 10: *Just for Fun*	220

INTRODUCTION

This book is all about making choices – looking at situations and deciding what to do. We are constantly challenged to make decisions – to select from a variety of options.

Not only in business and professional situations do we face choices, but also in everyday life.

Just think about the myriad decisions we have to make: time to get up in the morning; breakfast at home or on the way to work, or at work; what to wear; when to leave home; transportation by car, train, taxi, car pool, or walk; route to take; where to park, buy coffee, add a donut; start the day at the office, factory, store school, other.

Now it's time for lunch. More choices!!

Most of us don't think of these as "decisions" or "choices" but that's precisely what they are. Most of them are simple, routine, and safe.

But life is filled with complicated, expensive, and sometimes even dangerous situations requiring us to make decisions – and that can be difficult.

But consider this: no matter how complicated, confusing, and detailed a situation or problem is, ultimately, it boils down to a simple "Yes – No" decision.

Just think about that for a moment. Ultimately, every decision we make has only two options: yes – no, stay – go, add – subtract, try – avoid, up – down, etc.

The essays contained here revolve around such options. They explain and describe real situations in which choices had to be made because of circumstances.

As you read them, consider what else "could" have been done, what you might have done or avoided doing, and what consequences could have developed.

The book is divided into ten sections, but those aren't restrictive.

Please read them in any order you like because the sequence isn't significant.

Each essay is a "quick read," but hopefully you'll find yourself spending time considering the situations and implications.

Ask yourself a few questions:

What did I get out if reading this? What would "could" I have done? Was there an "Ah Ha" moment? Where? What was the "take away" for me?

I hope you enjoy the read.

For starters, look at this:

Change Your Point of View

Sometimes just changing the way we look at a situation makes it easier to see options and resolve issues, but many times we simply rely on old habits because that "old way" worked. Let's look at what can happen when we change a point of view.

Just for fun, and to make the point, solve this Math problem. I'm sure everyone can get the correct answer.

You are working at a tennis club. Management has scheduled a tournament. Singles competition, single elimination. One hundred twenty eight players have registered.

As the person in charge, how many matches must you schedule to complete the tournament and award a trophy to the winner?

To get the answer, most people write down columns of numbers: 64 + 32 + 16 etc. Then they add them up: That's how we've always done it.

The technique works, but if you change your point of view, there's another way. It's also much faster and less prone to an arithmetic error. You'll get the correct answer almost instantly. Here's the "new" way. Just answer these questions.

How many registered to play? 128

How many will win the tournament? 1

If 1 will win, how many will lose? 127

How many losers can you have per match? 1

If you need 127 to lose, how many matches must you schedule?

Of course, you must schedule 127 matches!

Done! Problem solved!

The "old way" works, but this "new way" is faster and more accurate. And it works with any number. With an odd number of players, you just post a bye, and byes don't require matches.

Now what does this have to do with business communications?

Plenty. Much of what we do and how we do it comes from habit. Because certain techniques have worked for us in the past, we tend to use them again and again.

Most people tend to focus immediately on the Problem – and the evidence that defines the problem. After that, they discuss the potential Solution.

Like the tennis tournament, this works, but there's another way. Audiences want answers and solutions; they don't want recitations of problems and lists of justifications. When a speaker focuses on problems, particularly at the start of a talk, audiences usually become impatient. They're waiting for the "So what" information. "So what are you (or we) going to do to fix this?"

At the start of a talk, audience interest is high. They are in the room or on the Internet to learn something. They usually already know about the "problem." They want the "solution."

Take advantage of that initial interest and provide new material. When speakers don't do that, audience interest and attention wane and may disappear completely.

The Point of View in any presentation should concentrate on what is important to the audience – Solutions – not Problems.

Remember this. To be a good speaker, think like a listener. Put yourself in the shoes of your audience, and it's easy to determine what they want. Tom Peters, the noted speaker and customer service guru said it clearly. "Find out what the customer (audience in a presentation) wants, and deliver it.

Such good advice is simple to articulate, but sometimes those old habits make it difficult to follow.

But, change your point of view, and presentations will be easier to construct and more effective to deliver.

Finally, many speakers immediately start making PowerPoint visuals. Don't do it. That's a good tool, but it might not be the "right tool" for your talk. With this revised point of view, let the purpose drive the technique.

Determine the tool by the reason for the talk and by the specific characteristics of the Audience. Picking the tool should be your last decision.

Again, put aside those old habits. Look at new options. See what happens.

See what progress you might make when you stick your neck out.

CHAPTER 1

Communication Skills

The key word in this title is "skills." And they relate to behaviors – to what people DO.

There are two major components to presenting material: Content and its packaging and delivering that content.

On the content side, presentations require structure. There must be a clearly defined start, development, and close. Audiences don't want to – and won't – wait.

If they don't get information quickly they will tune out and move on, either mentally or physically. Maybe both!

Either way, a presenter has lost them.

The other side is the presentation itself, the interpretation, the thoughts.

Audiences don't want just words; they want ideas; they want concepts; they want commitment; they want passion.

The following essays describe a variety of instances where words were supported by delivery.

Consider how those two concepts combined in the examples and consider what happened – and why:

That's Not Me – Or is It?

An almost universal reaction when someone sees a photograph of himself or herself is "That doesn't look anything like me!"

That's usually followed by others saying, "Yes, it does. It looks exactly like you."

Likewise, hearing a recording of himself or herself usually evokes, "I don't sound like that."

"That's exactly how you sound!"

The reason for the different perceptions is easy to explain and important to understand.

First let's look at the photograph. Most of the time when we see ourselves, it's in a mirror or other reflective surface. That result is an image reversed from what others see. When we look at the reflection, what is on the left side of the person in the reflection is actually on our right side.

The two sides of the human body are symmetrical, but they aren't identical. The reflection we see of ourselves isn't the same image anyone else sees. When we see a photograph, a motion picture, or a video recording, however, we see that "other" person the way everyone else does. Everything is in "the correct place."

As for the sound of the voice, there are similar reasons.

When we talk, we hear ourselves through two channels – air and bone. First, the sounds we make travel from our mouth to our ears, precisely the same way others hear us, through what is called "air conduction."

However, we also hear the sounds we make through the vibrations of the bones in our heads. That's called "bone conduction." No one else hears that sound the way we do!

When we listen to a recording of ourselves, however, we hear only what others hear – through the air conduction. Bone conduction doesn't apply.

We live inside a marvelous and complex system – our own body. It's important to concentrate on how it works, and, with a little thought, we can develop new skills to make that system work to our benefit. This is particularly important in business communication.

Start with this. Take advantage of simple and commonplace technology by recording yourself using commonly available audio or video devices.

Then look and listen to the results. Regardless of what you might think, that's how others see and hear you! That's the image you present to your various audiences during speeches, interviews, and even informal conversations. What they actually see and hear is more significant than what you *think* they are experiencing.

Don't argue with the evidence – use it.

Now it's time for assessment and honesty. Do you like what you see and hear? If so, fine. If not, ask yourself precisely what you want to change.

Here are a few questions to consider in order to "fix" what you want your audiences to see and hear when you talk to them.

Are you looking right into the eyes of audience members, or are you looking at the floor, the ceiling, the walls, or projection screens? Those things won't respond to you, but audiences will. Talk to people, not to things.

Be aware. – If you don't look at the audience, they might not look at you.

Are you standing up straight and still – the way your mother told you to – or are you shifting and "fidgeting"? A solid and balanced stance and posture will help you look professional and comfortable – even if you aren't.

Are you speaking clearly and with enough volume for your audience to hear you easily? If you aren't, they won't! Here's an unexpected benefit of increasing volume: you'll reduce the number of annoying non-words you use. Nice benefit.

It's quite possible that the first time you review those recordings, you might not be comfortable because you're observing someone you don't really know – yourself.

After you visit with that "stranger" long and often, however, you'll become comfortable with your new "friend."

Get to know that "stranger." Visit regularly.

When you do that, the professionalism will expand, and that's good for everyone.

Maybe you'll even be able to teach him or her a thing or two!

Don't Expect Your Audience To Be Patient

A while back, my wife, Eileen, and I were presenters at a Communications Seminar. We discussed material that has broad implications for many businesses, including these ideas which resonated with the audience.

When addressing any audience, remember: audiences are impatient.

They're polite, but they want something from you.

And they want it now!

Speakers often "ease into" a presentation by providing extensive background information. They want to "warm up" their listeners, but that's not what the audience wants, expects, or deserves.

After a brief "hello and welcome," get to the point of the presentation before the audience starts to review the agenda or look at the rest of the program events to determine what else they could be doing.

Capture an audience with a strong sentence that makes your point. Even if your point is "bad news." Make it quickly.

Here's an example: If the corporate offices are moving to Fargo, North Dakota, tell them up front. They might not like the news, but now you have a basis for a focused discussion. If you simply begin by saying something about relocating the headquarters and continue with justification for a move without stating the location, the audience becomes anxious, wondering when the "other shoe will fall."

Audiences want data, structure, and clarity.

Give it to them.

Speakers sometimes seem to take on the role of the mystery writer. They set up twists and turns, plant clues, and contrive surprise endings. That's good for the mystery writer. It sells books, which sometimes exceed five hundred pages, and readers devour them by choice, devoting hours to discovering "Who done it?"

But that's not the case with business presentations.

When offered an opportunity to talk about what you do or what your organization does, make your point with a few appropriate words like this.

"We build cars;" or

"We build safe cars;" or

"We build safe, fuel efficient cars;" or

"We build safe, fuel-efficient, eco-friendly cars."

Decide just how much information you want to put in one sentence, but car manufacturing is the primary point in each of the examples.

The focus is clear. If you use words such as "exciting" or "trend-setting," don't expect the audience to figure out what you want them to know. That's not their job.

Here's a disciplined way to make that all-important point quickly and clearly.

In one short sentence state what you do. Follow that with why you do it. And conclude with how you're going to do it.

Not only will this sequence get you started, but also it will open a dialogue by using the same questions and prompts to discuss: What can/should the audience members do? Why should they do it? How can they get started?

This compact sequence is important with business audiences, because many of them see themselves as "problem solvers."

As soon as a situation is presented, they immediately consider possible solutions. They have ideas about what could/should be done. Help them use that motivation to your advantage by framing the situation quickly.

By offering your recommendations you'll focus their thinking, but if you don't offer such information quickly, two possibilities might occur. First, you'll lose control and have to work even harder to convince them to accept your recommendation.

Second, they might "turn off" and follow a completely different line of thought. In each case, you lost them and the opportunity to direct and harness their interest and abilities.

Here's an exercise for you. As you plan a presentation, write down your answers to these questions:

What do you want your audience to know about you and your company?

What do you want them to do when your presentation is over?

What services can you provide for them?

What resources do you need from them?

What is the next step for them and for you?

Become a teacher, not only the speaker. Teach your audience what you want them to learn by helping them make your information their own.

And do it quickly.

The Power Of One

Every decision made in a family, an institution, or a company, a government agency or department can be traced back to an individual – a single person.

That person is the driver.

Without his or her initiative and direction, nothing constructive would happen.

In business and society today, we all become involved with teams, departments, and other groups; and often the people who constitute these groups discuss, debate, and compromise to collectively make decisions or plans.

But when we stop to think about the process, in every instance, a single person is responsible for the eventual decision and action.

No company ever made a decision!

No team or group ever made a decision. Individuals make decisions, and in every instance, a single participant is responsible for proposing an idea, focusing it, and moving toward an action.

Other participants agree to and participate in development; but without that individual driver, nothing gets started.

This recognition – and respect – for the power of one individual is significant because it can reduce the intimidation many of us feel in a variety of situations. Just realizing that one person – somewhere, in an agency or a company – developed an idea that resulted in a requirement or a regulation that has an impact on a business or an individual encourages us to raise questions rather than to accept new rules blindly, or just complain about them.

That's why group input has value.

As we navigate our business and civic worlds, it's important to remember the significant roles individuals play in making decisions, writing letters, and preparing contracts.

That means if you don't agree with a message and can substantiate your point of view, find someone of equal authority and work to get it changed.

Many people don't take that route because they are intimidated by a piece of stationery with an official looking letterhead. It's only a piece of paper.

Here's an interesting – and hopefully, enlightening – exercise. Identify a business or regulatory decision you think was really bad – or one that was really good.

Now, do some detective work. Find out who originated the idea. You may not come up with a specific name, but you'll see quickly that such a search will lead you to a single person. Even in a team action, someone will say, "Go!" Until that single person offers the direction, nothing happens.

There is always some*one* in charge.

Some individual person's "Eureka" moment is essential. Multiple people might be needed to implement the idea, but without the idea itself there can be no action.

And think of the implications a single idea can have. On the negative side, three decades ago, a major soft drink company changed its successful and profitable time-tested formula. But it wasn't the company making the decision. A single person developed the idea, and because of his stature and corporate power the formula was changed – with disastrous results.

On the other hand, many years ago a mid-west department store owner directed everyone in his company to, "Give the lady what she wants." That one man changed the course of customer service. His staff, of course, changed the way they treated customers, but he set the tone. He was the driver.

Not too long ago, we were able to observe an example of the Power of One in a fun way. On Sunday night, thanks to Abner Doubleday inventing the game, the Chicago Cubs faced the St. Louis Cardinals in the first game of the 2015 baseball season.

Then on Monday, most of the other Major League teams played their first games. But there's a problem. Sport history doesn't confirm that Abner Doubleday invented the game of baseball. Someone invented it, though, and huge crowds of people are glad he – or she – did!

Without that one person, none of us would have been able to enjoy the opening day or all the games to come throughout the season.

From the time we were little kids, we heard your name associated with baseball, and that's good enough for us.

So, thanks, Mr. Doubleday – even though the game wasn't really your idea.

Who Says So?

It's easy to intimidate or impress people. Just put on the cloak of an institution, and let it do the talking for you.

For example, when a letter containing bad news arrives in a mailbox, many people feel pressured to do something they didn't intend to do when they see the return address. However, taking a brief pause and considering the source of the information can make a big difference. Just look at these two sentences:

"The insurance company cancelled my policy."

"Charlie Jones cancelled my policy."

Which one is more likely to induce a panic response? The first one, of course, because it came from an institution.

But remember this. No institution ever wrote a letter!

Only a person can write a letter!

Here are a couple of examples demonstrating the power of the "anonymous author," and they raise the specter of having to "fight City Hall."

An acquaintance of mine told me how a letter from the Environmental Protection Agency (EPA) informed him he cannot expand his dock because of some new sea grass growing in the area.

A neighbor wants to build a patio in his back yard, but the zoning board wrote informing him it won't issue a permit.

Life becomes more manageable and less frightening, however, when we realize a missive was prepared by some person sitting at a desk somewhere. not by an institution or by an agency.

Since this "panic" response happens frequently, here's a suggestion that can help reduce anxiety. Find out who wrote the letter. Get a name and a phone number. Place a call, and talk to him or her. The Internet has made it easier to accomplish that task today than it was a decade ago.

It's impossible to talk to an institution, but it's easy to talk to a person. This is an important mindset, and it applies in many areas.

When I entered military service, a friend who served many years as a military officer gave me an interesting piece of advice. Initially I didn't believe him because it was contrary to everything I thought I knew about the military.

"During your service time you'll be subjected to many official orders," he told me. "Some you'll like;

some you won't. Of course, you must obey legitimate orders, but always remember, some enlisted clerk somewhere typed those orders. If you want to do something other than what the orders direct, find some other enlisted clerk who can legally type other orders."

When I was eventually in a situation in which it was appropriate to try out his advice, I did. It worked. He was right.

Here's another tactic that causes readers to react unnecessarily. Many institutional directives are written in passive voice, and read like this:

"Your policy has been cancelled."

"Your permit has been denied."

That wording alone is intimidating because it seems to be final and absolute rather than a "work in progress."

Well-placed questions about such sentences can often reverse a decision or modify directed action.

If and when you receive such a communication: first find out who wrote it; ask specifically who made the decision; ask why. You are entitled to an explanation. Worst-case scenario, you'll simply understand better the reasons behind the negative decision. Best-case scenario, you'll get that person to change the decision. That's well worth the effort!

"But wait, there's more."

As the legendary radio personality, Paul Harvey often said, "Here's the rest of the story."

When you are the one writing those letters, use these same tactics to your advantage.

Write in passive voice. Don't take personal responsibility for decisions or conclusions. Let the reader believe the directions are coming from a powerful impersonal source. The tactic will give you a distinct advantage.

By knowing how the system works, you'll be able to use it when you're sending a message, and you'll be aware of it when you're receiving one.

When all the players know the rules of any contest, the competition is always more interesting.

It's the Tone, Not Just the Tome

How clearly we communicate our ideas has a powerful impact on the success of our businesses, our family lives, and our civic interactions.

Many people spend long hours and extensive energy crafting and delivering messages. Others just "wing it." The first activity can be time consuming, but the second can be risky.

Either way, it's a choice, and there are consequences for choices.

Many people concentrate on WHAT to say, which is important, of course, but equally important is HOW they say it.

It's necessary to concentrate on what the receiver hears, and that's affected by a wide variety of vocal characteristics including: volume, pace, vocabulary, pronunciation, non-words, and tone of voice to name just a few.

On another front, written messages are also influenced by a number of characteristics, but we'll cover them at another time. Today, let's focus only on spoken messages.

Like many other behaviors, speech is a product of habits. We learn to speak by imitating sounds we hear from the time we are young children.

Some of us intellectually change and modify speech patterns and habits, but for the most part the speech patterns we exhibit on a daily basis are not planned.

Habits prevail, but we can't rely solely on those habits. We must make choices, and the first choice is to speak with purpose and deliberateness.

What an audience hears from us forms and influences what they think about us when they receive the information we deliver.

What an audience hears from us is far more important than what we say.

Think about that for a moment!

Our messages aren't for us. We already know what we want and why and how and when. Because our messages are for our listeners, what they hear should be of paramount importance.

We must take care the audience "gets" what we intend, and that requires planning. Not planning every word; that would take too long, and audiences would get lost. This planning focuses on the impressions we create.

How will our listeners feel about what we say to them? How can we construct that feeling? What tools do we have? How do we practice them?

Here is an often-repeated line that has been credited to a wide variety of people. So many I won't pick one in preference to the others. The attribution, however, isn't as important as the message. Remember this:

"People will forget what you said; they may even forget what you did; but rarely, if ever, will they forget how you made them feel."

Feelings are carried and remembered long after an encounter, so take care to create the ones you want.

Don't take a chance; take charge.

Use speech tools to your advantage.

Something as simple as the emphasis we give to a word can change the meaning of the words we say. This old song lyric provides sound advice, "It ain't what ya say, it's the way that ya say it."

Now, that's the lyric as written, but simply changing the slang words changes the feeling and the impression a speaker would create by using the "correct" words.

Going a step further and emphasizing just one of the words in the sentence changes the meaning. Look at these sentences, and listen to what happens:

It isn't what *you* say; it's the way that you say it.
It isn't what you *say*; it's the way that you say it.
It isn't *what* you say; it's the way that you say it.
It isn't what you say; it's the *way* that you say it.

Each sentence carries its own emphasis. Now do this. Say each sentence out loud. You'll hear even stronger differences. That's what audiences will get. They hear what we say out loud so that's what must be our guide.

Once again; it's risky to allow habits to determine how we voice our thoughts, because they can be misunderstood.

Audiences will remember the tone of voice we use as we address them, so be sure the sounds don't interfere with what you are saying to them.

Image Counts

The image we present to others has a powerful and lasting impact on our messages.
That was the final sentence of an earlier essay, and it's significant at the start of this one. Everyone with whom we have contact judges us by what we say and do. And because they do that quickly, it's in our best interest to have a plan for presenting ourselves in the best possible light.

And what we do influences how people assess what we say. One easily observed example these days is what happens when speakers use a TelePrompTer – that device that enables someone to read a prepared speech and seem to be looking into a TV camera or at a live audience.

I use "seem to" because that's the desired impression, but it doesn't always work. Like most hardware, using a TelePrompTer requires practice to become proficient.

Here are three suggestions that can make or break a speech read from the device – where the speaker/reader is looking, where the device is located, and how the speech is written.

First, where to look. Look directly at the TelePrompTer screen. This is particularly true if the speech is being televised. Doing that correctly will create the impression you are looking directly at your viewing audience – - if the device is positioned correctly. That's point number two.

For television transmission, the TelePrompTer screen, which is transparent from one side and displays the printed copy from the other side, should be placed directly in front of the camera lens. From the speaker's position, the copy is easy to read while the camera "sees through" the glass from the opposite side.

For a stage presentation place a separate TelePrompTer screen toward each side of the lectern. Read a bit of the message while looking at one of the screens. Then read the next sentence or thought silently. Move your eyes to the center of the audience, and deliver those words to the audience. Next move your focus to the other screen and repeat the sequence. This impression of making "eye contact" is important to engage the entire audience.

Point three – How the speech is written will also make an impact on your delivery. Write sentences to be "spoken" not "read." In most cases people speak in short simple sentences, but they write in long complex ones. Written vocabulary is usually more formal, too. Since you'll be talking to an audience, sound like you're actually talking to them rather than reading to them.

Reading a prepared text can present yet another problem for an audience. Remember when you were read to as a child? What was the purpose?

Right. It was intended to put you to sleep! And it still works!

Now, another word about words we use in business situations. Avoid jargon. It's interesting to note how quickly words enter the language. Here are a few that have grown popular recently.

OPTICS. METRICS. and PIVOT. They refer to what can be seen, what can be measured, and a specific point of view, but the words "see," "measure," and "perspective" take care of such meanings. Certainly there is nothing wrong with using the other words, but using them repeatedly produces the impression of having a limited vocabulary.

Don't risk creating that image by using the "one word fits all" words.

Finally avoid acronyms. They might be misunderstood.

A colleague of mine almost set off a major argument when he arrived at a meeting a few minutes late and heard the featured speaker recommending action that should be taken by the NEA. He was furious because he was convinced schoolteachers should not be involved in such activity. A moment before he sounded off the speaker said, "And that's why the National Endowment for the Arts should take that position." He had missed the full title when he was late for the start of the talk.

There is the NEA, and then there is the NEA!

We've often said, "Words mean things." Avoid the verbal shortcuts and potentially confusing acronyms. Use the appropriate words in order to create the desired image.

Image Might Be "TOO Good"

Many years ago a former neighbor of mine took over a business his father-in-law had started and developed into a thriving enterprise. Paul, my neighbor, inherited the business when the founder passed away.

The business was "personality driven" and required a great deal of one-on-one attention at client's homes and / or other social settings. Paul expected to continue growing the business, but he found his client base begin to erode.

Long-time clients and customers began to shift allegiances after long associations with his father-in-law.

He shared his concerns and his surprise with me about losing a sizable portion of his client base.

"I don't know what I'm doing wrong, but it must be something serious." He described what he did and how he did it, and an idea began to form in my mind.

Because I had known him for a long time and had a pretty good sense of what his answer would be I asked, "What do you wear to the client meetings??"

"Always a suit. I've acquired quite a work wardrobe even a step up from what my father-in-law had, and he often looked like he just stepped out of GQ Magazine. I think my appearance is very important to clients, and I have to look good."

With great pride, he showed me his wardrobe. Very impressive and very expensive.

My idea grew stronger and clearer.

Like most suburbanites, Paul had more than one car so I asked, "Which car do you use when you make your business calls?"

"The big one, of course. It's comfortable, and I think it makes an impression."

My idea was now fully grown, so I asked Paul another question.

"Could it be that you look TOO good and TOO successful to your clients? You're focusing on getting your clients to give you money for your services. Might it possibly look to them that you're getting too much money from them already? You look to be a lot more successful than they are when you drive up in that big car wearing that very expensive suit. Maybe you look too successful. Just a thought."

Paul ended the conversation saying, "I'll think about that."

Several months passed before we talked again about his situation. 'You might have been right about looking 'too successful,'" he told me. "I cut down a bit with the wardrobe, put away that gold chain and the Rolex watch, and left the big car in the garage. It might have been coincidence, but business is a lot better now, and I've picked up an impressive list of new clients."

I thought that certainly it could have been a coincidence, or it could have been a clear case of cause-effect. Sometimes we can display "too much of a good thing," as my mother used to say.

Customers judge us on many factors including appearance. It's worth looking at ourselves through their eyes from time to time, and asking ourselves, "What do they see, and how do they feel about it?"

Changing our point of view might change how we see ourselves. That, in turn, could change how customers and clients act toward us.

No one would ever argue that appropriate clothing and overall appearance are significant in business, but Paul's experience opens up a new view ? And a new question. Can something be TOO good?

A former colleague of mine often prodded his students with this comment. He said, "Any positive quality when taken to an extreme becomes a negative."

Just think about that for a moment. Borrowing from the Boy Scout Law, we

know that qualities like Trustworthy, Loyal, Friendly, Courteous, Obedient, Thrifty, and Reverent are all positive. Take them to an extreme, however, and they become: Gullible, Subservient, Obsequious, Fawning, Slavish, Miserly, and Fanatic.

It's a question of degree. When is enough enough?

Of course there is no visible line of demarcation between the positive and the negative labels, but the transition is worth considering as we interact with customers and colleagues.

But Not For Everyone

At the conclusion of a television commercial about a "significant breakthrough drug," I saw a comment that was either a powerful confession or a gigantic insult to viewers. It communicated the audience was either fooled, or stupid.

The disclaimer said, "Don't expect to achieve these results."

If a sponsor purports a product or service will produce specific results but doesn't get them, why market the product in the first place?

Or on the other hand, if the sponsors knew the stated results are questionable why spend the time, talent, and resources extolling its merits for any reason other than to fool gullible viewers?

There once was something called 'Truth in Advertising,' and it served as a first line of defense against dishonest claims. Advertising content was required to meet a certain standard of accuracy that seems to have disappeared.

Now the standard seems to be, 'Make all the claims you want within the body of an ad and then indicate at the conclusion that what was just disclosed might not be so.'

If a product is aimed at a large audience, what's the point and the truth in admitting it may be effective in some cases but not in all? And what's the purpose of spending most of the time on the "advantages" only to negate them in the final sentence? All too often, that sentence isn't even spoken. It's printed usually in small type at the tail end of a commercial.

It's there for legal cover. But the true purpose and the ethics are subject to question.

The real question isn't about confessions or insults. It's a simple Yes or No, without qualifiers. Does the product or service do what it is supposed to or not?

Here's another common qualifying statement. 'No case is typical.' After extensive claims are made in the body of the commercial the qualifier is tacked on to the content. And that qualifier negates the claim.

That tactic reflects an adage that seems to be popular in some businesses as well as in governmental agencies. It's the dictum that, "Viewers buy Image faster than they buy Content."

Think about the products and services and people that seem good at first glance but become tarnished upon careful inspection.

"Caveat Emptor ~ Let the buyer beware," is not only alive and well, but it has also become more significant as communication technology has expanded. Messages are packaged in ever-increasing formats and devices using highly sophisticated imaging.

Computer generated images are often impossible to distinguish from reality and we often see things that simply don't exist. Powerful visual messages are almost impossible to ignore and they are very convincing. Those images seem to be real, and they produce results.

"Seeing is believing" is no longer a reliable statement.

The general population has been so inundated by excessive claims that businesspeople must be careful of how products and services are projected. The impact of the bombardment is often a wiser, more sophisticated clientele. False claims and exaggerations become more obvious to observant viewers and readers.

When many people are deceived they become skeptical of claims. It's just sound strategy to avoid any appearance of saying what isn't so. Something as simple as claims that certain products advertised on television are 'not available in stores' is blatantly untrue. We see many of these products on store shelves every day.

It's easy to stretch truth or to make up facts to sell an idea or an item. Deception works for a while, but ultimately truth emerges.

In daily activities with customers, staff, and colleagues it's always best to maintain the high ground.

If we don't, we'll get caught, and there's usually a high price to pay for that.

As consumers, it's important to remember the adage, "If it's too good to be true, it is." The desire to want to believe in a product, a service, or a person can lead to misdirection and disappointment.

Be informed. Be skeptical. Be safe.

Hi Diddle Dee Dee, An Actor's Life For Me.

Let's begin with a couple of questions. (And a virtual show of hands to respond). First: How many readers are accomplished Shakespearean actors? Actor, by the way is the appropriate designation for both men and women.

Second: How many readers know someone who is an accomplished Shakespearean actor?

Probably only a few hands went up for each question. Why is that?

Almost everyone has access to all the scripts, and everyone can read and study the plays, so shouldn't there be a big response? Clearly, it takes more than the words of the script to be an accomplished actor. The words must be interpreted and delivered. How the actor brings them to life determines the impact of the play.

And now, another question. Raised hands aren't necessary for this one.

When businesspeople have to give a speech or make a presentation to clients or customers, how many of them give almost exclusive attention to the words? They write the words (their scripts), re-write the words, and then make some visuals that reflect the words.

Business executives in classes I teach admit they hardly ever rehearse! They're busy! Very rarely do they even say their words out loud until they are standing or sitting in front of their audience. Here's a thought for everyone planning to deliver any talk to an audience. Just because you have written some words doesn't mean you will be an effective speaker. As with the actor, how a presentation is packaged and delivered breathes the life into the words.

And just because an actor has a good script in his or her hands doesn't make that person a good actor. Likewise the businessperson delivering a presentation.

All too often businesspeople evade opportunities to deliver presentations. Many students at all academic levels also avoid giving presentations or "reports" as they are often called. Presentations can be opportunities to be welcomed rather than ordeals to be avoided.

Audiences at all levels judge us more critically on how we look and how we sound than on the words we say. Words are important; no one will deny that, but how words are delivered creates the impression and contributes to developing the convictions.

Here are some suggestions to help with creating those impressions.

First, talk to people, not to things. Look right at the audience's eyes, and talk to them. If you have to use notes or visuals, that's fine; just don't talk to them. They won't do anything for you, but people will.

Let your hands help you be descriptive. Don't lock them together, at your sides, or put them in your pockets.

Give yourself license to move. In daily conversation, everyone moves to describe and emphasize. Doing those same things during a presentation will make you look comfortable and confident. Audiences respond positively to such an impression.

Stand or sit up straight and balanced. Such posture tells an audience you are prepared and able to deliver your information. Move around when necessary and appropriate; just don't meander. That's a distraction, and signals to an audience you perhaps aren't the professional you know you are.

Finally, speak up so audiences don't have to work to hear what you are saying. There's an old adage related to volume that's worth remembering. "If you make an audience work to hear you, they won't." You lose!

Also, when volume is strong the voice isn't just louder; it's richer and fuller. It sounds like you're comfortable, which helps make the audience feel comfortable. Even when using a microphone, speak up. An amplifier will make you loud but not necessarily good.

There is an added benefit to using these skills. Those annoying "ums?" and "ahs" we hear so often will go away. When they are numerous, audiences begin to count them. When that happens, your potential impact disappears.

So develop solid content for a presentation, but remember the importance of the packaging and delivery of that content.

Like the Shakespearean actor, begin with a good script, and then rehearse, rehearse, rehearse.

A solid and professional presentation doesn't just happen. It's crafted.

Much Is Revealed When a Question Is Asked

We usually think of asking a question as a way to collect information and that works well. There's another way, however. Questions provide information simply by listening to the way they are asked.

If we listen carefully, even before anyone answers a question, the question itself can speak volumes.

In order to capture all of the information, though, it's important to listen to all three parts of a question. That's right, three parts, but most of us listen to only one part the words that are actually said or written. That's important, of course, but there is more than just that verbal part. Let's examine the other two parts as my co-author, Jack Grossman and I described in our book, *Becoming a Successful Manager.*

A non-verbal part is revealed by what is done while the words are being said. Listen for harmony or dissonance. Do the actions that accompany it reflect the words that were used?

The third part is revealed by how the words are said, the tone of voice and the words that are emphasized.

In the following sentences from employees to their managers, the words are clear, but other messages might be significant in understanding the real issues.

"Don't you think we already have too many meetings?"

"You're in charge. I'll do it exactly the way you tell me to."

"What do I have to do to gain some appreciation around here?"

"Why is it every time we schedule an appointment, you cancel it."

"I don't know if you realize it, but the only time I hear from you is when I seem to have done something wrong."

If you really listened, you heard the "hidden?" messages in each of these remarks.

So, one side of the coin relates to listening carefully to how questions are asked. Don't answer a question until you know what it really is. If someone asked you, for example, "Why are your prices higher than your competitors?" Watch out! You might go on the defensive if you answer this without getting more information.

You need to do some probing before tackling this one. Questions like: "Which prices?" "What product?" "What competitor?" These questions will help you specify the real issue.

Many businesspeople view themselves as "problem solvers" and jump right to a response, but, in this case, haste might lead to solving the wrong problem. Don't begin to answer any question before you know precisely what it is. A few questions of your own here will likely avoid lengthy explanations or verbal U-turns later.

Just as you want to be sure of the meaning of a question before attempting to answer it, when you are constructing your own questions, do so with care and clarity.

You'll get what you ask for, so be sure of your words and stay focused and accurate. If you were to ask a customer about the greatest difficulty he or she is having operating a new product, you'll get a laundry list of problems. On the other hand, if you ask a customer about the best features of a new appliance, you'll likely get a testimonial about benefits.

An old adage tells us, "Be careful what you ask for. You just might get it!"

Finally, remember questions open up routes for conversation. They identify what is important to another party – a customer, a colleague, or a family member. Don't view them as interrogations, but rather as requests for more information. Questions are like road signs. They provide direction. They aren't merely "Stop Signs" indicating "Danger" or "Rough Road Ahead." They give direction, speed, and location while offering permission or prohibition. They help us get where we want to go, but we have to be careful to understand them thoroughly.

A road sign is usually short, bold, and bright; but questions are sometimes confusing and convoluted, so give yourself plenty of room and time to process what the messages are.

And, by all means, don't begin your answer until you are sure of the question, and you're ready to begin your answer.

Proceed With Caution.

Fix It? – Or Just Accept It?

A new phrase has entered our everyday language. "The New Normal" Like any other living language, English is constantly changing, but sometimes changes sneak up on us. We find ourselves using words and phrases we never expected to come out of our mouths.

Sometimes they speak volumes about us "for better or for worse" about our outlook and about our expectations.

All manner of new procedures in employment, education, travel comfort, living standards, and financial security; to name just a few, are now referred to as "The New Normal."

In almost every instance, however, that label describes an unavoidable lowering of standards, expectations, and services.

The phrase demonstrates a willingness to blindly accept a significant downward change without question. It says that although something isn't as good as it once was, we just have to get used to it.

The impression is: "If it's Normal it must be okay. Even if it's inferior, it's okay because it's Normal."

That's self-deception, because whatever is defined as "normal" then becomes normal.

Accepting such thinking provides an easy excuse for giving up. It justifies surrender.

A disturbing element of the phrase is the potential impact of simply accepting without question that something is inevitable. It says, "I can't do anything about this. I'll just go along so I can get along. Ever hear that before?

It encourages defeat.

That defeat, however, is the result of the fact that language can change behavior. Words influence and shape belief.

This "New Normal" is the latest version of some previous popular aphorisms including:

o It is what it is,

o Accept the inevitable,

o Que Sera, Sera ? Whatever will be, will be.

When we hear something repeated often enough, we find ourselves falling into the trap of believing it. Repetition can build the façade of truth, and if listeners don't question the idea the words evoke, behavior changes.

That's what often drives advertising? The slogans, the rhymes, the jingles, and the frequency. Political campaigns have used this technique for ages, and it and works!

A carefully selected and focused short sentence, when repeated often enough shapes, our thinking, and can eventually change our behavior. In extreme cases, the technique has been called, "The Big Lie." History is filled with examples so we don't have to repeat any of them here.

So, be careful about the level of credence we give to such comments. Also, be careful about what we tell ourselves. For example:

Remember the time you were invited to a social event, and you told yourself it was going to be boring, and it was? On the other hand, how about the time you went to an event after telling yourself it was going to be great fun? It probably was!

Language influences attitude, and attitude influences behavior.

Avoid telling yourself or letting others convince you changes are unavoidable and inevitable because something is "The New Normal."

It's possible you might not be able to change everything you want, but in your own best interest, think of the sentiments and the directions included in what has been called "The Serenity Prayer." Written by the twentieth-century theologian, Reinhold Niebuhr, it has had a far-reaching impact. Aside from the religious community, it has been adopted be Alcoholics Anonymous and other twelve-step programs, and it was also distributed by the US Army and the USO in Germany after World War II.

Consider the power of these words:
God, grant me the serenity
To accept the things I cannot change;
Courage to change the things I can;

And wisdom to know the difference.

In our business and personal lives it would do us well to weigh these thoughts before accepting the notion of "The New Normal."

Assess a situation, gather facts, and evaluate options. Then select the course of action most appropriate for you and for your business based on facts, not on feelings, and certainly not on a new catch phrase.

You Are the Most Important Visual

Seems that almost everyone who delivers a presentation these days uses visuals. Today, it's PowerPoint. Years ago it was thirty-five-mm slides in a Kodak Carousel Projector. We've all moved up in the "High-tech" world.

Presenters use them because visuals are powerful, and they can carry a great deal of information. Sometimes they carry too much information, but that's for another time.

In a previous column I suggested that visuals should be made only after the content, sequence, and audience have been defined, and I stand by that. But, let's assume you've done that, and you've created good visuals.

In most presentations there is another visual that doesn't get much attention.

YOU! You are the most important visual in your presentation.

The audience observes – and evaluates – everything you do, how you do it, and how you look when you're doing it. The first impression they get should be carefully crafted and executed.

That doesn't imply being deceptive, but you must be aware and discriminating.

In a moment we'll visit some physical skills to use in presentations, but first, let's take a brief look at your appearance – your clothing.

This won't be a fashion review; just a look at what should be common practice and obvious. Unfortunately, much of it is neither.

For both men and women, common sense must prevail, but factor in these considerations. Make sure the clothes fit properly: not too tight, not baggy. Nothing provocative or flashy. Everything must be clean and pressed. Go easy on jewelry. It can be distracting, and it can interfere with items like microphones and remotes.

I know, for some, I'm stating the obvious; but presenters sometimes don't realize the impression clothes create and how they influence the audience's impression.

With so many levels of business dress these days, be sure you know what kind of environment you're entering. Is the dress code, "business," "business casual," "casual," or something else?

Once I went to a meeting where the dress code was "business campus." I had never heard of that, so I made a few phone calls and learned it consisted of t-shirts, shorts, and flip-flops.

Be sure you know and conform to the code, and then dress slightly on the high side of it. That can be tricky sometimes. (Think "business campus.")

I have a business associate who is proud of how he dresses. He usually looks like he stepped out of a fashion magazine. That can be good, but he realized his version of what that meant became a serious problem for him. His four-figure suits, alligator shoes, gold rings and watch were creating a "big money" image. Many of his customers thought they must be paying too much for his services, and? "excessive" profits were going into his clothes closet. Eventually, he eased back on the pricey clothes.

Remember, it's all about the audience. Consider what they'll think about you, and respond accordingly.

Other factors to consider concerning you being the most important visual include these behaviors. Before you say the first word in your talk the audience is already evaluating you. They process all of this information.

How do you walk to the front of the room? Fast? Slow? Hesitating?

How do you organize your material on the table or lectern?

Where do you look as you're getting ready?

Is your stance even and balanced?

Do you make eye contact with members of the audience?

Do you engage your audience by moving closer to them?

Even though you haven't yet said a word you've sent many messages. Everything you have done will influence how the audience will react to what you say when you start to talk. You have already set their expectations.

Throughout your talk, continue to be aware of your appearance because the audience certainly is.

Remember, you are the most important visual in your presentation.

Impatient Audiences

The adage tells us that, "Patience is a virtue," but in many instances audiences don't demonstrate that quality.

Makes no difference if it is in a large auditorium or in a boardroom, an audience wants information "right now." And the higher they reside on the organization chart, the less time they'll wait.

In order to perform well in such a pressure situation, have a game plan.

We've all heard the advice about, "Tell 'em what you're gonna tell 'em. Tell 'em. Then tell 'em what you told 'em."

That's been around for a long time but it seems lately that a different approach might be appropriate. An approach like this.

For starters: "Tell 'em." Right away. That's why they came to the meeting in the first place. They want to know what you're recommending. It's interesting to note that even if the audience doesn't agree with what you're saying, they want to know about it right away – no matter if it's good news or bad news they want it now!

Next, "Tell 'em" why you are delivering your specific point. What is the justification for your recommendation?

As soon as they've heard the news they'll want to know why, so here's the place to tell them.

Many speakers want to take time at the beginning of a presentation to provide a "Set up." Especially with bad news speakers are tempted to "ease into" the bad news. When that happens audiences quickly become inpatient. If a speaker withholds the news too long, the audience becomes annoyed, and that can be a serious problem.

So, begin with "What." Then quickly follow up by telling them "Why."

Immediately, they'll know your position and hear your support for it. No time wasted here.

The third step is to tell them "How" you intend to accomplish the task.

In coaching sessions, we often use the analogy of a legal trial as an example. In a trial, each attorney begins by stating his point: "Find my client innocent" from the defense. "Find the accused guilty." from the prosecution.

The members of the jury don't have to "again figure out" the position of each attorney.

The next phase of a trial is each attorney presenting evidence to prove his or her position – guilt or innocence.

Again, the jury members don't have to figure out if specific pieces of evidence are good or bad news for the accused. Each attorney tells them!

Imagine how complicated it would be for jury members to have to figure out if specific evidence was good news or bad news for the accused.

In the third step of a trial, the attorneys provide the marching orders to the jury and tell them how they want them to proceed to closure.

This is precisely how a presentation should unfold. Tell the audience: What you want, Why you are making the recommendation, and How you recommend it be accomplished.

This format is fast, clear, and specific. It's also possible to add background information to the "Why" section if time permits or an audience member asks a question. Be sure to keep answers to questions focused on the recommendation, and avoid being forced or tricked into talking about other issues. Staying focused on the topic is easy if you simply refer back to the recommendation by saying "That's why I'm suggesting…"

Stay focused, and honor the time demands of your audience. Don't stretch their attention span. It might snap back and hit you.

Make your point up front. Audiences look for such focus, and they appreciate such attention. And always remember, as we've often said before, a presentation is for the benefit of the audience, not the convenience of the speaker.

So test this format. See how it works for you

CHAPTER 2

Managing Techniques

In early employment years and entry-level jobs most of us were "Doers." We learned what to do, how to do it, and we were rewarded by how well we did it.

When we did well, we got promoted to another level, and we learned how to do more things. This cycle was repeated until we reached a fork in the employment road, and we became a manager. Congratulations!

No longer were we doers – or we shouldn't have been. We were now responsible to get others to do the work. Our job was to guide, teach, coach, and evaluate their performance.

The difficulty was this. For the most part no one taught us how be a manager – to get those others to do the actual work.

When things went wrong, we tended to retreat to past behaviors. We jumped in, and we fixed the problem.

In short, we became doers again. But that was no longer what we were supposed to do!

When we "Jumped in" like that the others for whom we were responsible didn't learn or grow. They were simply "place holders" because we didn't guide them.

It's difficult to be a Manager, but these essays present some ideas that merit your consideration.

Think about how you might have responded to the situations – and the benefits of "managing" rather than "doing."

Old habits die hard for all of us, but there are some solid suggestions here.

They might work well for you.

First, The Person

Well. We're already into the second week of a new year! Traditionally this is a time for new beginnings. We celebrate and look forward to events and changes. But sometimes there are endings that must be recognized.

In business settings such changes surface in products, procedures, and people. Nothing stays the same, and the changes require attention and care.

It's probably a pretty good guess that many readers have been in positions to guide, manage, evaluate, and even terminate employees. Let's start the New Year by revisiting techniques that can help navigate those difficult waters.

Perhaps the most important – and difficult – task of a manager is providing guidance to those for whom he or she has responsibility. Because a manager can't and shouldn't attempt to DO everything, it's necessary to teach staff what they need to know and to coach them as they develop.

A manager should be a good and sensitive teacher. That requires attending to each individual in the "class – the department or the company. The most powerful activity in any instructional environment isn't "teaching," however. It's "learning."

The student, the staff member, the participant is the one who must internalize new information and adopt new behaviors. The manager provides the direction through information and criticism – constructive criticism.

As we turn the page to a new year, with the holiday season" in the rear view mirror, think of that constructive criticism as another "gift" still to be delivered.

Constructive criticism is indeed a gift, but to be viewed as such, it must be properly wrapped and sensitively presented. In order to determine how to provide constructive criticism it's important to first become that other person, and focus on that person in order to determine the most appropriate action.

Here's a simple example. Put yourself in the position of someone who reports to you. If that person did something "wrong" you have at least these four possible responses:

Ignore the action;

Chastise him or her in private or in front of colleagues;

Tell him/her what was done wrong but offer little or no help; or

Call attention to what was done wrong, determine the cause of the error, agree on a course of corrective action, and determine what needs to be done.

Of course, the last action is what you would want because it calls attention to an error, but then it allows you to become part of the solution.

Although this tactic works, many managers don't apply it. They confuse criticism with adverse judgment. To assure that constructive criticism will be the dominant message, remember these points: Criticisms are gifts; When delivering those gifts, be specific about what is needed and expected; Deal with the error, not the emotion.

An additional factor relates to offering the gift of constructive criticism. The personal relationship inherent in any exchange of gifts grows and develops over time. A trust factor plays an important role, and here is where "the person" comes into play. In reality, at least two people are involved – the manager and the employee, or employees. It is also important to restrict the conversations to the individuals involved. As soon as other people are within hearing distance, the relationships change. The "gift" being presented is a personal matter. Keep it personal. And confidential.

Most physical gifts are given at specific times of the year: for birthdays, weddings, and other celebrations, but constructive criticism shouldn't be confined to specific dates and times like scheduled performance reviews.

Many people dread them – managers – for having to conduct them and employees for having to participate in them. But think about this:

A Performance Review should be a process – not an event.

If a relationship has been built over time and included open communication by all parties, by the time the "official performance review" date arrives (most organizations have then) there should be no surprises for any on the participants. And there will be none if the manager encouraged and nurtured a continual cooperative working relationship.

When that happens the Performance Review will certainly be a process – not an event.

Try it.

Hiring the Wrong People

At a recent conference I heard a business executive say something to which I and many other participants responded with great surprise. Here's what he said – loudly and emotionally.

"All the people I hire these days are no good! They never stay very long.

Those two sentences spoke more about him than about his hires and short-term employees.

Hiring an employee is a difficult task if you don't have a solid game plan, so here are a few factors to consider. Of course, there isn't only one way to accomplish that daunting task, but here are some time-tested steps.

First, be sure you know precisely what you need. What skills, experiences, and personal traits will be required? That sounds obvious, but it is often overlooked. When you think you know what you need write it down. Don't just "think about" it. And be specific about what you write.

If you can't write it down on a blank piece of paper or on a computer screen, you probably aren't sure of what you want. It's impossible to fool a blank page or screen.

Taking the time to write out what you are truly looking for will save you a great deal of time later. It will also save expensive hiring and training time and dollars.

Once you are sure you know what you want from a new employee, check the applicants by using this three-step process.

As an instructional vehicle we're going to compare the hiring process to climbing a mountain, and we'll call that process ALP. The letters stand for Able, Likely, Personal.

Step one: Able. Determine if the candidate possesses the skills and knowledge to meet the job requirements. Much of this information will be relatively easy to secure by close examination of the applicant's resume?. This is all past tense and it's easy to review. Carefully look for gaps, lapses, or omissions. If you find any, make a note to ask about them during an interview – if there is to be one.

That takes us to the second step: Likely. What is the applicant likely to do if he or she is hired? This is future tense, so assess what reaction you can expect concerning future activity, growth, and willingness to learn new skills that direct and contribute to the growth and health of the company.

Be prepared to ask questions during the interview that will uncover such needed information. Share your questions with others in the company who will likely participate in the interview process. The interview is the best place to compare the past activities with the future needs.

Of course, be aware of the legal limitations and restrictions about what you can and can't ask or you might find yourself the respondent in an uncomfortable inquiry of another type!

The third element is perhaps the most difficult one. It's the Personal element that will determine the probability that the applicant will "fit into" the existing workforce and corporate structure.

Again, have other colleagues participate in the interview process in order to assess the likelihood of such compatibility. Once a hire decision is made it can be difficult to undo an error.

These aren't hard and fast rules to this process, and interrelations need to be flexible in order to assure success. For example: a missing skill (Able) can often be overcome with sufficient training (Likely). On the other hand, solid skills and a willingness to learn may be overshadowed by a negative personality (Personal) that can destroy a working relationship.

So look at the entire process. Ask the applicant – and yourself -- the tough questions. And by all means, be sure of what you want and need so you'll be able to see it when you're looking at him or her!

Keep that alpine analogy in mind. With planning, instruction, and effort, a climb to the top of a mountain is rewarded with a beautiful view and a sense of accomplishment. Taking a short cut or making a misstep, however, will likely lead to little more than a fast trip to the bottom.

Modifying Managers

While working recently with a major US based international corporation, I was reminded of a concept my wife and I have observed with many of our clients. It is both sobering and exciting, and the first question that comes to mind is: "How can something be both an "upper" and a "downer." Seems contradictory, but it isn't. We'll focus on business experiences here, but it affects everybody in every walk of life.

Here's the concept: Everything is changing – all the time. That's exciting for some people, frightening for others. Many of us avoid looking at that certainty and the emotions that accompany it. Some changes move quickly, some more slowly, but the changes do come. Nothing today is the same as it was yesterday; and tomorrow it will be even more different.

Some changes reflect and demonstrate improvement, some just the opposite. It depends on how we embrace or reject change.

This isn't intended to be a depressing idea. Quite the opposite. It is intended to evoke a positive reaction. It is an invitation to explore how we relate to our own individual worlds and to the people in them.

All too often and as a matter of self-deception, we behave as if they will always be there. Think again!

Constant change has enormous implications for how we conduct business, and, in fact, in determining what is happening to our businesses, our customers, and our associates.

Many organizations, large and small, are currently recognizing the need for "retraining" their workers. To the surprise of many, those workers include managers and C level personnel.

Over the years, with increasing frequency and speed, the ways of doing business have changed and cannot be managed the same way now as they were a decade or two ago.

Many of today's managers and C level personnel, however, were "trained" to run businesses and specific departments under conditions that no longer exist. Their training no longer matches their responsibilities.

Even the word "training" could be revised. Many professionals now prefer to use the word "teach" or "educate" because those words reflect human behavior.

Animals are "trained" to perform certain tasks in specific ways. They don't measure, plan, revise, and select appropriate actions based on acquired and evaluated data.

Unfortunately, the word "re-education" has taken on negative and sinister definitions because of various political and literary references. (Remember George Orwell's *1984*?)

Regardless of the word that is used, however, even experienced staff members, managers, and other leaders must learn new specific elements of their jobs because many of the "old ways" are no longer operational.

Managers must learn new ways to relate to today's new employees. The "new" people are responsive to factors far removed from those of twenty years ago.

It's incumbent on today's managers that they learn – again – how to manage employees. The operational rules of the game of business have changed. Some current managers might not like that, but to remain effective, they must learn new skills, or they may become obsolete.

Learning new rules and behaviors doesn't mean the old rules are now bad. They are just different! A sport analogy might be appropriate here.

An accomplished athlete, as talented as he might be, cannot play quarterback on a baseball team. In order to join a baseball team, he must learn a new set of rules and skills. A great baseball pitcher would need to relearn how to throw a ball if it were to morph into a football. He might still be a great player, but he would need to acquire and apply new behaviors.

As the game of business changes, so must the players change in order to "stay in the game."

It just makes sense for professional managers to update and use their abilities and drive to avoid being sent back to the "minors" because they couldn't "cut it?" any more.

So, here's the instant re-play: Everything changes; people, products, technology, rewards, opportunities, goals, tools, challenges, etc.

Maintain your values and your focus, and learn the new game.

Who knows? You might even like it better than the old one.

The Extremes Are Easy

One of the most difficult parts of being in charge of anything is the need to make decisions. The manager of a business, the principal of a school, a teacher, or a parent is required to make judgment calls on a daily basis.

Even what seem to be "routine" events are the result of unique characteristics that are influenced by a vast variety of variables including changing times, individual participants, operational pressures, and interpersonal relationships. In other words, no two events are the same. And that poses a problem for the person in charge.

In recent years a wide variety of institutions and organizations have adopted a "fast track" approach to decision making. The approach has many names, but the most common is "Zero Tolerance."

When an observable event takes place, a single element is used to identify "what happened," and the characteristics mentioned above become unimportant and irrelevant. When only that single event is deemed to be significant a reaction to it is simple.

It's almost like using a checklist where Column A indicates the element and the corresponding Column B dictates the response. Using such an approach enables anyone ?"n charge" to make a quick decision without having to think because, once the element is defined, the corresponding reaction is predetermined.

All the variables become unimportant. The consequences reflect a "one size fits all" mentality.

What otherwise would require thought, analysis, and judgment is simplified and catalogued in the pages of a discipline manual. Just look up the event, and Presto, the dictated response pops up.

No thought is needed to make the swift decision. No time is wasted thinking, analyzing, or judging.

The interesting factor here is this. The desire to organize and codify reactions to events does have some value. Clearly articulated systems can produce efficiencies.

However, as I mentioned in another column a while ago, my colleague Jack Grossman was correct when he wrote, "Any positive action, when taken to an extreme, becomes a negative."

Think about that for a moment. A disciple becomes a zealot; desire becomes compulsion; guidance becomes domination; thrift becomes miserly; and caution becomes cowardice.

As soon as anything becomes "All vs. None" or "Always vs. Never" there is no room for assessing individual situations – what some would call "common sense."

Recently a magazine published a story that describes this "Always vs. Never" limitation. A nine-year boy established a mini library on the front lawn of his home. A sign on the little blue box on red stilts read, "Take a book, leave a book."

He did it to promote reading, and no money changed hands, but the local government shut him down, citing an ordinance that bans "structures on front lawns."

That was certainly zero tolerance in action because it focused on a specific element and provided no room for interpretation.

His little box of books was a structure, but it likely was not what was intended when the statute was written. But, once written, no one had to think about it anymore.

Another recent news story describes how an elementary school student was suspended for "terrorist activities." His offense? After seeing a movie with his parents, they gave him a souvenir ring similar to one used as part of the movie plot. When he went to school he told some of his classmates, "With this magical ring I can make you disappear." That "threat" resulted in his suspension.

The school principal justified the harsh reaction by saying, "We can't tolerate threats to other students – even fantastical ones."

Certainly the intent of both examples was sound, but taking them to the extreme in each case made them almost ridiculous – made then negatives.

No one will dispute that rules and boundaries are necessary, but being "in charge" requires evaluation and judgment not simply the ability to read a manual and select a response. True leaders and true managers are decision-makers, observers, evaluators, and not just good readers.

Responding to "extremes" is easy, but understanding the variables that surround events requires careful thought to be valid and positive.

Groundhog Day – Again

Groundhog Day has been around for more than a century, and the lore indicates that a groundhog named Punxsutawney Phil will come out of his hibernation spot and predict the weather. If he sees his shadow, winter will last another six weeks, but if the day is cloudy and he sees no shadow the weather will be moderate, and winter will be over.

It's a fun story and a festive celebration each year, but old Punxsutawney Phil hasn't been very good at the prediction business. The predictions have been correct only thirty-nine percent of the time – not very good from a business perspective.

But, here's another side of Punxsutawney Phil and Groundhog Day. In 1993, Harold Ramis directed a motion picture with the same name. He and Danny Rubin wrote a story in which a TV weatherman relives the same day over and over, and, of course, that day is Groundhog Day.

We're looking at it here because, at the moment, it seems in many areas of business and society, we are doing what has already been done. For example:

Businesses rise and fall based on the same factors they experienced in the past. The success/failure of schools, likewise, ebbs and flows, and educators work at researching multiple factors aimed at solving the same problems they faced a generation ago. Social and race related situations also continue to demand attention.

The pages on the calendar have changed, but the attitudes and behaviors haven't. It's Groundhog Day again.

In many ways it seems we haven't learned from our past actions, and the results are predictable.

To paraphrase George Santayana, those who don't learn from their past experiences are doomed to repeat them. In many respects, it seems that each generation is determined to make its own mistakes and to think it is traveling in new territory.

If businesses operated that way, they probably wouldn't be in business very long. Businesses look for solutions and developments, not opportunities to revisit old problems, point fingers, or just "try again."

Here's an interesting way to examine a "problem" be it business, academic, civic, or social. First, look at this definition. "A problem is a perceived divergence between a reasonable need or expectation and what has or is currently happening."

Since the perception belongs to the person with the problem, the problem belongs to that person as well. And that is a key factor in resolving any problem!

Solving a problem doesn't come from simply assigning guilt and finding fault. It requires collaborative effort. All parties have to participate in order to move from the perceived gap to what is desired.

Without the willingness to share the identification of the cause, there will be no success in finding a workable and agreeable solution.

Having a positive attitude and a true desire to understand why the problem exists and what is causing it provides a direction and a strategy for remedying it.

You can't always fix the cause, but knowing what the cause is provides insight into figuring out how to remedy the problem.

In both the annual groundhog event and the movie, there were no positive actions. Events were left to chance. When Punxsutawney Phil wakes up, he may or may not see his shadow, and that happenstance is credited with determining if weather will be good or bad.

In the movie, Phil Connors, the TV weatherman, just goes to sleep at the end of each day, and the morning delivers unplanned activities and events.

In neither instance is there any direction, focus, control, or intent.

Waiting for things to change, improve, or expand is precisely what both "Phil(s)" demonstrate, and neither one can take ownership or credit for anything that follows.

So, as we continue to face business, academic, civic, and societal problems and opportunities, take ownership and set courses.

We've done many of the same things over and over again when they didn't work in the first place. No point in trying them again just to look like we're "trying."

Don't Water the Weeds

While driving out of state recently, I heard a guest on a talk-radio program make an interesting comment about using talent and resources well. I don't remember the program or the entire discussion, but I do remember this one-liner. I like one-liners because they deliver strong messages with an economy of words.

He said, "Don't water the weeds."

Just think about that for a moment. With all we have to do in business, it makes no sense to waste time, talent, and resources cultivating weeds rather than focusing on the flowers.

I think that line resonated with me because in, *Becoming a Successful Manager*, (McGraw-Hill) a book I co-authored with my friend and colleague, Jack Grossman, we described these three major roles which define a good manager: Be an Effective Teacher; Be a Sensitive Counselor; and Be a Master Gardener.

I'm sure I reacted to that radio comment because it reflected the analogy Jack and I used in describing some of the qualities that contribute to being a good manager. Here's some of what we said about managers being good gardeners

If anyone were to ask a serious gardener to describe the secret for success the response would be something along the lines of, "First, I have to create a fertile culture that stimulates healthy plant growth. Next, I must ensure that the different species of plants in the garden are compatible. And finally, I have to maintain the garden by watering, cultivating, weeding, and fertilizing it, and by providing special attention to the plants that require it."

Master gardeners will also say this is a full-time job yielding great joy when they see the positive results of their efforts.

It doesn't require much of a stretch to apply the rules and principles of successful gardening to being a successful professional manager. The "human plants" you select ? or inherit – to be part of your business garden must reflect your values and be willing to contribute to your vision of what you want your garden to produce. Your abilities and skills will determine how productive and responsive they will be. The chance of managing a cooperative team that's full of potential is great if you do your job well.

But, a significant part of your job is to see to it that "weeds" don't drain your business garden of its nutrients or adversely affect its productivity.

Of course, a business garden consists of people, who are much more complex than varied flowers and vegetation. However, they both require fertile soil as well as proper care and feeding in order to flourish. Some people, like exotic flowers, may even require special treatment.

Regardless of their differences, what's obvious about both gardens is that neither can be taken for granted if it is to flourish.

And this attention is a constant process. Most of us have experienced what happened when we left a garden unattended for an extended period because of vacation, travel, or a host of other reasons.

When we return, the weeds seem to have been on steroids in our absence. They have far outpaced the other plants, and in some cases, have "taken over" the garden. That requires hard work removing the weeks just to get back to where we were previously. We do it with the plants, but because it isn't so easy with our "people gardens" we often delay. When that happens, the roots grow deeper, the weeds grow stronger, and the removal is more difficult.

Sometimes weak or corporate gardeners "transplant" the weeds to other locations, but that doesn't solve the problem. It only defers or transfers it to another gardener.

As a manager, as with the master gardener, select the plants carefully before adding them to your garden. If they "came with the job" examine them quickly to assess their quality.

Nurture what fits – remove what doesn't.

A garden can't fix itself. That's the gardener's responsibility.

And remember, as that radio guest said, "Don't water the weeds."

I Don't Mean To, But…

Sometimes people say and do things just the opposite to what they intend – or purport to intend. And they say and do those things without giving thought to the comments or the actions. Here's what I mean.

With great frequency we've heard – perhaps even offered – comments like: "I don't mean to interrupt, but…" or "I don't want to disagree, but…" or how about this? "I don't mean to change the agenda, but…"

I'm sure we could add more, but this should make the point.

In every one of the above examples, the speaker did indeed interrupt, disagree, or change the agenda!

The habit seems to be an attempt to excuse away bad behavior. The intentions of such speakers and the outcome of their comments are clear to everyone who knows them, but the speaker gives himself or herself permission to behave inappropriately.

Here's the other side of such behavior. The person who has been interrupted, disagreed with, or forced to revise the agenda is equally responsible for the behavior because that person allows it to happen. That person is an "enabler."

Think how interesting it would be if the "I don't mean to…" comment were met by, "Then don't!"

That would certainly be a conversation stopper at a meeting, a conference, or a business discussion.

Isn't it interesting that one party has no qualms about "taking over" a situation, while the other parties surrender to the offending party?

Here's another contradictory sentence. "You'll never believe this, but…"

If any speaker thought that was true, the comment would go unspoken. No one would want to waste time and effort saying something no one would believe. Of course they expect their listeners to believe their comments.

Here's one we observe every time there is some kind of celebrity award ceremony like the Academy Awards or the Emmy Awards. "I never expected to…"

When the winner in a particular category is announced the celebrity walks to the microphone and recites this line. "Just being nominated is an honor in itself. I never expected to win." Then he or she takes out a prepared statement and reads the names of everyone who was helpful in the production.

If there was no expectation of winning, why prepare the speech? One could admit to hoping to win and therefore being prepared just in case, but saying I never expected to win can be seen as pushing humility a bit too far.

We've heard businesspeople – especially entrepreneurs – say, "I didn't think this would work." It's hard to believe such a comment because if that person didn't believe it would work, it would never have been attempted in the first place.

Many have heard business colleagues proclaim, "I wasn't sure I'd ever be able to get the funding for this, but…" People, especially businesspeople, don't waste time, resources, and effort on concepts and activities they think will fail. Such behavior just doesn't fit their personalities.

Those self-deprecating behaviors and comments might evoke images of the stereotypical farmhand with downcast eyes kicking dirt and saying, "Aw Shucks."

It just doesn't make sense, nor does it create a positive and professional image.

Better to be positive and to take the initiative with comments like, "I have to interrupt to correct the minutes," or "I must disagree with that comment," or "The schedule has to be changed to accommodate the revised shipment," or "Listen to this new development," or "I'm honored to have won," or "From the start, I knew this would work," or "I knew the funding was out there somewhere if I looked hard enough."

When such words are delivered with the appropriate tone of voice, eye contact, facial expression, and body language the impression is strong and positive. With inappropriate delivery, however, the comments are judged to be self-centered and arrogant.

The outcome depends on the choice of the words and how they're delivered.

As we've said in the past, "Whatever you do – do it on purpose, in order to create a professional image."

Fight or Flight?

In business activities, most of us strive to be supportive and inclusive. We focus on fostering cooperative and mutually beneficial outcomes for our customers and our colleagues, and we offer products and services they need and want.

That just makes good sense. That's what business relationships are all about.

So why is it many of today's messages that confront us are foolish and even violent? Think about some of the examples you've seen on television, and ask yourself, "Would I ever do or say that to a customer or a co-worker?"

Usually, the answer is a definite, "No." Why then are such tactics used by some businesses to sell their products and services when the messages don't reflect the real would?

Many people try to avoid conflict and confrontation – sometimes to their own disadvantage. (If people don't defend a position, the resulting neutrality can be interpreted as timidity and uncertainty.)

In an effort to be seen as neutral they attempt to "keep the peace." If that's what many people do, why then do so many speakers and advertisers assume the posture of conflict?

Every day we hear speakers telling the world they will "fight for a cause, a position, or a product"

Politicians are prone to declaring how they will "fight" for constituents when they never lift a hand or make a fist. They don't "fight" for anything. The word sounds strong, and its use conveys determination, but it's hollow.

The word creates an impression that constituents have elected a modern-day gladiator or "knight in shining armor." Neither is true. There is no "fight." There is only "talk."

We see the pseudo bravado in other venues, too – most notably as mentioned earlier in relation to television advertising. Violence is almost everywhere in TV commercials not to mention the programming itself. Collisions, explosions, and demolition are integral elements in many commercials. People and things break other people and other things in a very-not-so-safe world.

For the most part, the world is a relatively safe place populated by decent people. Commercials, however, don't seem to be filled with those "nice" people. Many of the characters portrayed are foolish, naive, silly, or just plain stupid.

Is that just a case of attention getting, or is it how the writers and producers see their theatrical world? Good theater portrays unusual behavior because that makes for solid story lines. Commercials, however, aren't theater. Far better if they related to authentic behaviors in order to entice viewers to become customers.

"Cops and robbers" stories are popular because they provide exciting vicarious experiences, but commercials are intended to change viewer behaviors, and that's not make-believe.

In commercials, fathers are often foolish, mothers are usually muddled, but children are always champions. If the real world met those criteria we would probably live in a perpetual state of chaos.

Now, if commercials deliberately depict a fantasy world, why would anyone expect viewers to believe what they see and hear and then spend their money to acquire the offered product?

Sometimes, even "serious" commercials have surprise endings. That's especially evident with pharmaceutical products, which show "normal" people but conclude by making unexpected and sobering statements like, "Actual results may differ," or "Could cause serious side effects, including " (Insert your own calamity.)

The products often depict heartfelt stories, but then they make it clear to viewers that the product might not do what had just been described! Strange behavior.

So, what's the point of all of this for business? Simple. Tell the truth in a manner appropriate for real people. Tell your true story – not the fiction.

The advertised products and services have value so stress that. Focus on "contributions" not on catastrophes.

Solid relationships will be strengthened and preserved by helping viewers make good decisions,

A basic principle of communication states: "To be an effective presenter, become your audience."

Audiences are real people who make real decisions about real products and services. They aren't caricatures or violent cartoonish characters. Showing respect results in getting respect.

Working With Negative People

Because it's so easy to do, many of us tend to put people into categories -friendly, pleasant, interesting, annoying, negative, etc. Once we mark them with a label, we tend to respond to and act toward them with an almost automatic response.

That seems to make our lives easier because we don't have to think much about how to respond. But it can cause problems if "those people" are Negative People (NPs). Let's look at what might make sense as we navigate through our workplace contacts with NGs, because working with negative people can be draining. That drain can be costly because it distracts us from our business focus. We need a plan. So how do we stop – or prevent "negative and pessimistic people from poisoning our workplace and our relationships? If you manage or work with an NP, here are some suggestions to improve the situation and the relationship.

First recognize this is a "Toxic Behavior" which will worsen the longer it is allowed to continue. Take time to understand why the person is negative or pessimistic.

The behavior developed over time- not overnight, and no one can fix it with just a few clever statements. Certainly, Confrontation won't fix the situation, but Communication will. So here are some steps we can take as managers to address that negativism.

1. Ask Questions. We don't know what's causing the bad attitude so find out before trying to address it. The cause could be fear of failure, lack of necessary information, unfamiliar processes, adjusted reporting relationships, not feeling part of the work team, or a host of other reasons. Don't assume you know the cause. Ask about it!

2. Listen to the Answers. Really listen. Don't just wait and nod your head in agreement. You might learn about factors you never considered – factors that shape the problem and define the person. If you don't listen, you can't expect that other person to listen to you.

3. Discuss options. The "negative person" (NP) just might have some good ideas. You're still gathering information so be sure not to stop the flow of information. You might not know all you need to know yet.

4. Agree on Possible Solutions. Encourage the NP to articulate what he/she believes should be done. Don't you do it. When the problem person describes what is to be done, it's more likely to happen because he or she "buys into' the solution. Behavior is much more likely to

happen if the NP suggests the solution. Of course, you have to agree with it ? It's a two way street.

5. Assure that he or she is specific about actions, timing, expectations, etc. Without specificity there can be no accountability. Write down answers to these questions. What will happen? When? Who will do it? How will everyone know when it has been done? What will be the consequences if it isn't done?

6. Touch Base. At regular agreed-upon times meet to evaluate progress – or lack of progress. Changes in negative behavior require time and attention. Permanent changes won't happen after just a single meeting.

In *Becoming a Successful Manager*, (McGraw-Hill) my co-author and I used this analogy. A workplace is similar to a garden in which the plants, the soil, and the nutrients require constant care and attention. Without attention from the gardener, the weeds take over. Negative people are human weeds and require attention or they will take over the garden. They might have to be removed from the "workplace garden."

To maintain the productivity and stimulation of that workplace garden, look for the early signs of potential trouble because awareness is the beginning of change.

Everybody has a "bad day" from time to time so don't overreact to one of those. Be supportive where necessary because everyone you meet is fighting some kind of battle. A consistent pattern of negative behavior, however, is the giveaway. And that requires action because weeds don't monitor themselves.

Go After the One Who Did It.

I'm not sure if it's just because I've become more aware of this behavior, or that it's becoming more commonplace in business.

I'm referring to the "grammar school punishment" of all students in a class because of the misbehavior of a single individual. Often, in those situations, the identity of the "offending party" is unknown. "Someone" did "something," and the entire class is punished.

I became aware of that last month when a colleague told me about his manager who called for twenty-one experienced professional employees to participate in a required conference call. The reason – a client had "heard" complaints about the behavior of an individual "someone." There was no indication of time, place, action, or personal identification.

Here's what he told me. The manager sent a two-page email to the entire twenty-one people so they could prepare for the conference call although it contained only vague references to the "someone comments.

All twenty-one were criticized, but the offending party (or parties) wasn't contacted directly. No one had specifics.

Criticizing an entire group for the alleged "infractions" of a few is terrible management!

In *Becoming a Successful Manager*, my co-author and I stated: a manager is a teacher and a leader. A manager faces unacceptable behavior immediately and directly.

Writing accusatory emails and requiring attendance at a subsequent conference call is weak managerial behavior, and it demonstrates incompetence.

My colleague continued: The critical email sent prior to the conference call ended with an attempt to make everyone happy by closing with this statement, "Thank you for the tremendous job you do." It was like addressing children rather than competent professionals, and it was as inappropriate here just as it's inappropriate and ineffective in a grammar school classroom.

After two pages of criticism and accusations, the concluding sentence of that email made the entire communication laughable.

The manager wasn't doing his job, and was alienating his entire staff by making unfounded accusations based on lack of information.

There is an axiom in business circles that states when solving problems first isolate behavior and then be specific about it. That way a manager won't create even greater problems by reacting to "wrong" information.

As bad as the email was, the conference call was worse. The manager began with a rant saying, "This has got to stop. This will not be tolerated. This must change. This cannot continue."

The problem with those admonitions was the simple fact he never defined what "this" was.

There were simply vague references to what "Some clients overheard." As the call continued, the pitch of his voice heightened, and the volume grew louder.

Talking with some of the call participants later in the day, my colleague confirmed the general reaction was insulting. The people being chastised had no idea what caused the concern in the first place nor did they know who had done what to whom.

Further, because no specifics were presented, they had no idea what "had to change."

Although this conference call involved almost two dozen people, aside from the manager, only a handful had anything to say.

The others felt it was impossible to contribute to a diatribe when the direction was so unclear.

The call ended abruptly and surprisingly when the manager informed all the "offending" participants that, "But you are great. We talk about you to our clients all the time. You are the face of the company. Thank you for all you do."

Talk about confused and confusing messages!

From time to time, every company confronts difficult situations, but correction requires clarity, accuracy, and professionalism. Responsible adults expect and deserve to be treated as responsible adults – not as errant school children.

It's quite possible that manager was dealing with his own problems. That might have contributed to his behavior, but he didn't resolve anything. In fact, he wounded his relationship with his staff.

My colleague concluded that only time would tell if it was a critical wound.

The Other Side of Rights

Recently, both print and electronic media have been focusing on the wide range of "Rights" we have as citizens – and as businesspeople.

Many across the country agree that some of our rights may be threatened, and their arguments deserve our attention because of the consequences such a development would have.

Rather than becoming enmeshed in any specific debate, however, I want to look at "Rights" from another perspective – one that doesn't seem to get as much attention in business circles as many think it should. That's the other side of "Rights" which is "Responsibilities."

At the risk of sounding like a variation of Newton's Third Law of Motion, think about this: "for every Right, there is an equal Responsibility." All too often, however, people demand the "right" but disregard the "responsibility." Why is that?

That attitude seems to reflect a self-centered personal philosophy. One is about receiving something for which no effort has been expended, and the other requires contributing something and working to produce it.

I thought about this recently when I read a report on the increasing use of company-owned computers to carry on personal activities during the workday.

That's not why anyone gets hired.

When someone enters into a work for pay relationship that clearly indicates an agreement between parties to devote a specific amount of time and effort in return for a specific amount of money. That's a simple concept that defines the "two-way street" of a work relationship.

Regardless of the location on an organizational chart, it is understood that every participant is expected to work for the duration of the workday.

To accept payment without working for it is theft.

Most people would never consider stealing funds from a company they work for, but many never consider the implications of stealing time.

People are using company computers, cell phones, etc. for strictly personal reasons, but they are accepting full pay while engaged in non-business activities.

Workers are paid to work – not to shop on line or correspond with friends via email.

It's important for all us to remember that just because something is possible doesn't mean it is permissible or acceptable.

Workers certainly have the right to use company equipment. That's part of their job. But they also have the responsibility to use it for the purpose intended – company business.

That's the "quid pro quo"

Just as we all have the right to drive a car, we have the responsibility to obey the laws. We have the right to vote, but the responsibility to be well informed about issues. In the current public debate, we have the right to own guns, but we also have the responsibility to use them safely.

Considering this relationship of Rights and Responsibilities is particularly significant at this time of year when we recognize President's Day on Monday and remember the contributions of two of our greatest presidents. Washington and Lincoln were both focused on securing the rights of citizens and engaged in great and costly conflicts to protect those rights and assuring they endured for future generations.

Both men accepted the great responsibilities thrust upon them to do what they considered to be the right things to preserve, protect, and defend our society.

So this week, while honoring both of our former Presidents, it's appropriate to reflect on the Rights-Responsibilities relationship in our business dealings and in how we use and protect what is available to us.

No question about it, we have the Right to work under safe conditions, but also we have the Responsibility to deliver all the services for which we are paid.

Sometimes it's difficult to buck a trend in the workplace because of peer pressure when "everyone else is doing it," but with resolve, it's possible.

In the words of Abraham Lincoln, "If you think you can, you can; if you think you can't, you're right."

In business, as well as in society, in order to preserve the rights we enjoy, let us always take our responsibilities seriously to preserve the rights we enjoy.

Behaviors Have Consequences

Whatever we do during the course of our business – and personal – days, produces reactions from our customers, colleagues, and social acquaintances.

Many of the behaviors are unintended, and daily pressures sometimes cause them, so here's an idea that might help avoid inappropriate reactions.

Attitude is a powerful factor that influences our behavior and how we view situations and conditions.

Consider this definition of attitude my co-author and I used in our book, *Becoming a Successful Manager*.

"An attitude is a state of mind and a predisposition to action based on what you tell yourself.

"Attitudes precede actions; positive attitudes lead to productive actions; negative attitudes lead to unproductive actions."

From the book, here's an example showing how attitudes work, and how what we call "self-talk," can provide control and direction:

The customer-service department of a Midwest company was receiving frequent complaints. Specifically, people said customer service representatives treated them rudely. They were left on hold for what seemed to be forever, disconnected while waiting to be helped, and then not given the help they hoped to receive.

These complaints had gone on for almost a year and were accompanied by a steady decline in sales. During a meeting we had with the five-person department, we asked, "When the phone rings, what do you tell yourself before you answer it?"

We received blank stares and no immediate responses. With some encouragement, though everyone eventually related a variation of the same negative self-talk comment. We heard, "Here comes another complainer!"

After discussing the effect self-talk can have on behavior, we suggested they tell themselves something else when the phone rings. For instance: "This caller has a problem. My job is to help him or her to solve that problem, and I can do that. I'm a valuable resource to this person in trouble."

As part of the solution, they also adopted the greeting, "How can I help you?" when answering the phone.

This simple question was more than words. It was a genuine positive attitude, revealed in their tone of voice that said, "I want to help you."

Within a month, the vice president of operations started receiving feedback praising the customer service department.

The lesson learned was this. If your attitude is negative, it will come through; but if your attitude is positive, that, too, will come through.

This positive attitude suggestion isn't a "magic bullet" that will solve all your problems immediately, but it will go a long way influencing and reshaping behavior. It's a kind of self-fulfilling prophecy.

We've all done this to ourselves without even thinking about it. There may have been a time you were invited to go to a meeting you didn't want to attend but didn't have an option. If you chose a negative attitude and told yourself the meeting would be a waste of time, it was. On the other hand, if you had chosen a positive attitude and told yourself "This is a tight time, but as long as I have to go, I'll see if I can learn something I might have missed out on had I not been invited, you did.

In all likelihood whichever attitude you choose will result in your prediction coming true. When we have a strong belief about the outcome of a relationship or an impending experience, we do everything in our power to make that belief come true.

It's a pretty safe bet to say that attitudes are responsible for creating and perpetuating our successes and failures as well as the quality of our relationships.

Business is all about building and maintaining relationships, and directing attitudes by this self-talk can be a great help for all of us.

I've written this line before:

People might forget exactly what you say, and they might forget precisely what you do, but they will never forget how you make them feel.

Use this "self-talk" technique. See how your attitude can shape your behavior.

To Avoid Disappointment – Lower Expectations

When my wife and I lived in Chicago the running joke about "Da Cubs" was, "If you don't expect much, you won't be disappointed." A close second was, "Wait until next year." And we always did!

In spite of these comments, fans continued to purchase tickets, and Wrigley Field continued to fill up. The good feelings inspired by the "mystique" perpetuated the support.

In business, however, performance trumps feelings. Businesses must perform, or they go out of business because good intentions never overcome poor behavior. A NASCAR vehicle, for example, never won a race because it had a great paint job. That may make the car look good, but other factors make it a winner.

In business, we expect people to do what they're paid to do. Performance is crucial. That seems so obvious some readers might be wondering, "Where is this going?"

Here's where. Because education institutions provide the eventual workforce for all businesses, what those institutions do has a profound impact on the cost of doing business.

With increasing frequency, educators are telling us about the evils of "teaching for the test."

Many people across the country, however, ask, "What's wrong with expecting students to pass a test to demonstrate they have mastered specific material?"

Before earning a driver's license, everyone must demonstrate knowledge of the rules of the road by passing a standardized test. Lawyers must pass the bar exam in order to practice. Doctors must pass exams before they are board certified. Engineers have to demonstrate mastery of multiple skills to be sure bridges don't fall down and airplanes stay up in the air.

The educations for those professionals rely on the ability to demonstrate proficiency by passing tests. That's much smarter than assuming proficiency because they sat in a classroom for a specified number of hours.

So what's wrong with teaching the facts and concepts students must have, and then requiring them to demonstrate proficiency? After all, if they become cashiers, they'll have to be accurate every time they make change in a store. (Had a cash transaction in a store lately?)

If they're taught to "think," but they can't "compute," what have they learned?

A test is simply a way to assure someone has mastered content, and there's nothing wrong with teaching that content in order to achieve mastery. Knowing "how" to add a column of numbers is fine, but getting the right answer is absolutely essential.

In a "former life," I was dean of a teacher-education program at a small college with an "Open Enrollment Program." Applicants could enter the program without demonstrating basic abilities.

I remember one particular meeting where faculty members were criticizing the lowered quality of many entering students. My comment to them was simple and clear. "We have no control over the abilities of the students when they enter our program, but we have total control over their abilities when they leave us.

"The only way we can be sure of that is to set standards and test to assure students meet those standards – not just help them to "feel good" because they 'tried hard.' It's all about performance."

If students aren't required to demonstrate performance, why should businesses hire them, teach basic skills, and add to their own cost of doing business?

When testing shows that students can't perform what is expected of them, it makes no sense to make the tests easier by lowering the standards. That's avoiding disappointment by lowering expectations. No one is fooled, and everyone loses.

I'm reminded of the old joke about a patient who couldn't afford to pay for an operation, so the radiologist re-touched the X-rays.

It's easy to lower expectations, but the cost will be high.

We must be sure our businesses, and our employees, are capable of providing quality service to our customers.

Moreover, unlike the Chicago Cubs, businesses can't afford to "wait until next year.

CHAPTER 3

Customer Service

Most of us have experienced instances when "Customer Service was an oxymoron.

All too often we seem to forget that they are the reason businesses and jobs exist. Without them everything disappears.

Many of us have seen customers as "interruptions." We're busy doing something, and they expect – sometimes demand, attention and assistance.

When our focus id disturbed, it's clear to see that. When our attention is directed, it's clear that providing good service is easy – just as easy as providing bad service.

In a word, poor customer service makes no sense. Remember the adage: "If we don't take care of our customers, our competitors will."

The events in the following essays describe some good, and some not so good examples for your consideration.

Take some time to review and to consider these events.

What could have made the situations better?

What would you provide as an appropriate suggestion?

How can we teach ourselves to provide better customer service?

Everyone's Job

Customer Service isn't – or shouldn't – be a department. It should be a state of mind.
And it's everyone's job!

That really means "everyone" from the corner office on the top floor to the back room.

Here's a brief story to illustrate the implications and consequences.

In a "past life," I worked with an organization that specialized in the food industry. At one of our annual meetings, the president of the association jolted the audience of senior executives in attendance with this comment. (It was a while ago so these aren't his exact words, but they're close, so I'll take the liberty of using quotation marks.)

He looked at the group and said, "All of you in this room run very profitable companies. During the past year your companies handled millions of dollars, but your customers don't know you. In addition to that, no one in this room handled any 'real' money! You got spreadsheets and financial statements.

"The people who handle the real money are the least paid, least trained, least valued, and least respected people in your organization – the clerks and cashiers.

"To the customers, however, those people are your company. How they relate to your customers dictates how your customers think about you.

"What messages are they delivering to your customers? What are they doing to and for your customers? What services are they providing?"

His remarks relate to every business.

Good customer service is simple. Many volumes have been written and training sessions offered about it, but good customer service can be summed up in five words. "Treat people well – as individuals." That's it.

Customers come into your place of business to give you money. Be nice to them because they have a great deal of power.

Sam Walton made this clear when he said, "There is only one boss. The customer. And he can fire everybody in the company from the chairman on down simply by spending his money someplace else."

No matter what business anyone of us is in, someone else offers essentially the same product or service. Customers buy the people they encounter, not just the things, and they'll shop where they are treated well.

Be helpful, and take the extra step. For example, when a customer asks for assistance, resist the temptation to just say, "It's in aisle 7" or "Go down that hall, and turn left. You can't miss it."

Differentiate yourself by saying, "Come with me. I'll show you." Then take the customer to the appropriate spot. It will take you only a few moments, but the customer will remember it for a long time.

In some of the most successful companies in the country, that behavior is central to their customer service policy.

Be sure your entire staff follows that practice. A few extra moments with a customer can lead to a long-time relationship. Because it's the little things that often develop customer loyalty, give the customer more that he or she expects.

An old adage in business tells us, "People might forget what we said to them, but they'll always remember how we made them feel." Make them feel special.

So far, our focus has been on face-to-face service, but we would be remiss if we overlooked phone service – or lack thereof. Think how your customer feels when a machine answers a phone call requesting assistance and is then forced to navigate through a menu as complicated and convoluted as an Indiana Jones treasure map.

The machine says, "Your call is important to us," but then, as Rodney Dangerfield said, "We don't get no respect." We wait, and we wait!

Because all business is person-person, good customer service can be simple.

The legendary retail store owner, Marshall Field, had it right when he said, "Give the lady what she wants."

If we don't take that simple step, our competitors will.

What Do Relationships Really Mean?

Every day in our personal and business worlds we're faced with challenges, opportunities, and choices. Some of them we like and pursue; others we avoid. The difficulty is selecting the appropriate options.

Many of us are prone to make decisions immediately. Some in the work force do that because they are sure their experiences have taught them what is correct and appropriate. They reflect on past activities and success rates, they select those same options again.

Seems like a sound practice, doesn't it?

Others in today's workforce, however, have less experience, but a great deal of self-confidence. Their peers, who have similar opinions and experience, often reinforce such self-assessments and influence decisions.

Their reaction becomes the proverbial self-fulfilling prophecy. "I think I'm right and good. You too think I'm right and good, so it must be true.

"Therefore, what I think and recommend must also be accurate – and good."

Many decisions and debates between such groups within the workforce are related to one of the popular buzzwords receiving attention today: "relationships." There is much discussion about the importance of building relationships whether it be with individuals within these groups or with customers, vendors, or other colleagues.

It seems to be a generally accepted and important element for doing business. But what is it? How do we build it? How do we keep it? And how can we nurture it?

First of all, relationships are very personal, and they require attention and commitment from all involved parties. They involve much more than just "doing business" over an extended period of time.

Relationships involve more than spending time in an office or on a golf course, buying lunch, and asking about the kids and the family pets. A relationship might begin that way, but if that's all there is, it dies quickly.

True relationships require Individuals to "give a bit of themselves" to another person.

When defining and describing a true relationship certain concepts and words come into play. It's impossible to define such relationships without including these concepts: trust, concern, care, and support.

Perhaps that first word, "trust," is the primary ingredient in building a true business relationship. Without trust, it's difficult if not impossible to believe what is said or promised. When the parties can't believe what they are told about price, quality, delivery, forecasts, opportunities, etc., the interaction between parties can become confrontational rather than collegial.

Comments may be challenged until proven. Conversations that are parsed and footnoted often include comments that reflect a "Yes, but…" framework.

There is little doubt that successful businesses revolve around offering a product or service in turn for receiving a mutually agreed upon payment of some sort.

A good relationship also reflects concerns for another party to the point where they demonstrate care and support whenever it's needed, not just acknowledgment when it's convenient. It's the personal demonstration of truly "being there" when needed and not just being present.

It results in true and open communication and an honest exchange of ideas, not just giving directions, taking orders, or "doing a deal."

Developing relationships in business is a willingness to enter into a long-term personal interaction with others as equals. Each party contributes and receives support on the basis of what is needed, not just balancing an imaginary scale or keeping a scorecard on who owes what to whom.

Building a true relationship makes us vulnerable because we agree to provide honest comments – even when they might be negative. Sometimes things are bad or wrong and need to be corrected, not just accepted or, worse yet, overlooked completely. To not provide such feedback diminishes the potential of the relationship and could even jeopardize future business.

But, it takes strength – and courage – to offer such comments.

Kermit the Frog told us, "It isn't easy being green," and it isn't easy to develop a true and lasting business relationship.

But when we do, the results expand our businesses – and our worlds.

That's pretty good payback for the efforts expended.

To Thine Own Self Be True

When the Bard had Polonius tell his son, Laertes, "To thine own self be true," he was also sending a message to every businessperson, parent, teacher, and public figure to "Just tell the truth."

In the line following that advice he presented the reason and the justification when he added, "And it must follow, as the night the day, thou cannot then be false to any man."

Recent news items have carried many items describing how that simple advice has been ignored. There is no way to know for certain that is the result of a general decline of honesty or an increase in the access to information through expanded use of communication media.

This isn't a judgment about the current state of honesty and morals because most of us follow that other advice from Matthew 7:1 "Judge not, that ye be not judged."

It is, however, an observation about how we relate to colleagues, peers, superiors, subordinates, and family.

That relationship is also illustrated in the language we use.

It has been said that to be a good liar, one must have an excellent memory because it's difficult to remember all the intricacies of a falsehood. Truth, however, is transparent – and consistent. Either something IS or it ISN'T. Simple, clear, universal.

Because the word, "lie" is such a strong, harsh word our language has willingly accepted the use of other words to explain away or to smooth over the lies.

We see and read news stories about how someone "misspoke" or "misremembered." Sounds as innocent as tripping over a new rug. It communicates, "I didn't intend to do or say that; it just happened. It isn't my fault."

But when anyone "misspeaks," that person is indeed responsible because the action was deliberate, and it was intended to influence a belief or an action. He or she plainly lied!

Another word has gained some notoriety lately in relation to not telling the truth. "Embellishment" has been used to explain – or justify – telling a lie.

An old adage in communication tells us "Words mean things." But words can also deceive. For example:

Reading that a service offers a "discount up to fifty percent" can be an attractive lure because we see the number. The "up to" words, however, clearly indicate that might not be the actual discount! That discount might be only one percent.

A product might be advertised for a specific price "as is." That's an eye catcher, but the actual price might be much higher. Those statements aren't lies, but they do deceive.

A corporate representative promoting an event recently stated, "We donate one hundred percent of all profits to charity." Sounds wonderful, but profit is what's left after paying salaries, expenses, incidentals, etc. There might be nothing left, so the charities would get nothing.

Products are sometimes touted as "having a value of..." Again that sounds enticing, but who establishes that value?" The amount could be anything the writer says it is.

When clients and customers come to us for purchases or assistance they are placing their trust in us. They are expecting us to be honest and straight forward – and they have a right to expect that from us.

If any businessperson plays a "word game" with customers, it might work for a while, but sooner or later the TRUTH will come out, and the language impact will be clear.

"Double talk" doesn't last for long, but it's results do!

I've mentioned my first-grade teacher in previous columns, and her advice is as sound today as it was decades ago. "Say what you mean, and mean what you say."

Those nine words can serve to ward off the need to explain, justify, clarify, or correct a lie. And it's easy, too!

Polonius was right, and so was Sir Walter Scott many years later when he wrote, "Oh! What a tangled web we weave when first we practice to deceive."

Our customers and colleagues expect – and deserve – honesty in every interaction. There is never a good excuse for not providing it.

Time is a Treasure

With a tip of the hat to the lyrics of the old British folk song, "The Bunch of Thyme," in all business dealings it's important – essential – to remember, "Time, it is a precious thing." Everyone is allocated a specific amount of it, and it makes no difference if it's used well or wasted. When it's gone, it's gone.

When we waste time, we can't put it in a plastic bag and set it on a shelf to use another day. Time is non-renewable, so it's important to honor it.

Everyone's time is equally important, but that's often overlooked in many business, civic, and social settings today. All too often the hierarchy in various organizations ignores that simple fact.

It's easy to see that abuse. Think of instances when you were called to a meeting scheduled for nine a.m. You were there at the designated time, but the convener wasn't. He or she called the meeting, but then didn't arrive on time, so everyone had to wait.

There will always be unavoidable situations, but we all know the careless and habitual latecomers. Unfortunately, even though we can usually predict their behavior, we find ourselves having to tolerate a situation that might inconvenience us.

That's rude, and it borders on arrogance and disrespect. In many instances, it's just a bad habit, but it's still arrogant – and it wastes valuable resources of a business. It's difficult to justify making otherwise productive people sit in a room waiting for the convener to arrive.

As more and more meetings are now held virtually, that waste spreads over increasingly large geographic areas. So when we schedule a meeting, it's incumbent upon us to honor and respect the selected hour. That's one of the unique factors about time. It's specific! Noon is noon. It isn't 12:04 or 12:27. It's 12:00.

Another time waster is the person who takes more time than is allocated on an agenda. When anyone goes beyond the allocated time, an equal amount of time is stolen from the following participants.

During a discussion of this topic in a communication seminar I taught not long ago, one of the participants – an Executive Vice President of a large corporation – proudly made this comment. "Whenever I participate in a program, I make it a point to be the first one on the agenda. That way I can take all the time I want!"

A low groan rippled throughout the room. He showed his disrespect for others, and he was arrogant about it, too. In the vernacular of the day, "He just didn't get it."

Misuse or disregard of time can just be a bad habit, but it also can show lack of planning, forethought, or attention.

Everybody's watch works the same way and at the same rate of speed, but I heard an interesting explanation

– or excuse – for not honoring time. The excuse relates to the ever-increasing use of digital rather than analog timepieces. With digital timepieces, the numerals change, but everything still looks pretty much the same. With an analog clock, however, the image is constantly changing, and the minute hand keeps moving closer and closer to the all-important "zero hour." A fast moving second hand makes the picture look even worse!

Analog timepieces demonstrate that time is constantly moving, and that's an interesting visual lesson and reminder. Very few things in life, and in business, are certain, but time is – so it demands we pay attention to it. Use it well.

Also, it's important to respect other people's time as much as we respect our own. Available technology can help with that recognition. With a simple phone call – or text message – we can alert others when we'll be late for a meeting. They can then adjust their personal timetables and use their time profitably until we arrive.

Anyone, regardless of the position on the organization chart, can cause time waist. Don't be that person because, as we said earlier, once it's gone, it will never come back.

Indeed, "Time, it is a precious thing."

Guidelines vs. Rules

Sometimes well-intentioned, well-thought-out, and sound decisions become rigid and inflexible restrictions. The result is usually absurd or annoying – and difficult to justify.

In most businesses, regardless of size or focus, managers are expected to make decisions and offer recommendations concerning how the business operates; who does what and how it is done. Sometimes the why – the reasons behind the are explained. But not always.

Frequently, items that start out as suggestions and recommendations become hard and fast operational requirements. Options give way to restrictions, and interpretation and flexibility disappear.

It's easier for an employee, for example, to say, "The boss says…" than it is for that person to assess the conditions surrounding a situation and make a judgment – to make an independent interpretation.

Here's an example I learned about recently.

When a prospective customer entered a hotel restaurant for an early dinner while on a business trip she was greeted by a smiling hostess.

To the customer's surprise, the restaurant was empty except for one couple sitting in a booth at the rear of the room.

The customer said, "A table for one, please."

The hostess responded, "How about a booth?"

"No," the customer replied. "I prefer a table."

"Tables are reserved for large parties," the hostess said.

"But there isn't anyone in the restaurant except for that one couple."

"I can seat you at a table outside on the patio," the hostess offered.

"It's very chilly out there, and reports say there could be showers. And there are lots of tables right here inside."

"Tables are reserved for large parties."

The volume level went up when the customer repeated, "But there are no customers here – no parties large or small. The restaurant is almost empty. I prefer to sit on a chair at a table not to slide into a confining booth."

Once more the hostess said, "I can seat you at any of the tables outside, but the inside tables are reserved for large parties. Let me direct you to a booth."

With firmness and even more volume the customer repeated, "I prefer a table, a table inside this empty restaurant."

The lone couple smiled and nodded as the situation became increasingly ridiculous.

The hostess finally said, "Okay, this way please," and she seated the customer at one of the many empty tables.

What probably caused this encounter was a manager providing a sound suggestion that tables could be used for large groups because it's easier to serve large groups seated at a table than crammed into a booth. That makes sense.

What didn't make sense was the hostess's rigidity. She took the manager's suggestion as an absolute restriction and avoided making a judgment based on the realities of the situation: early evening, no other customers, a chill in the air, a possible shower, and a customer's stated preference.

The result of this encounter included: the couple in the booth was amused, the hostess was annoyed, and the customer was frustrated.

What an unnecessary conclusion to an ordinary situation – an early dinner at an empty restaurant.

Certainly, rules and regulations are important in every business, but so is common sense. It's doubtful the manager who decided that tables would be reserved for large parties intended the unbending restrictions to apply to a single customer in an empty dining room.

The initial direction was logical, but the unbending application of that direction was not.

Giving the hostess the latitude to make a decision based on circumstances would have eliminated the problem and contributed to a pleasant meal that evening rather than a debate and a conflict.

To that customer, that hostess was the company, and illogical rigidity was not the intent of the manager when developing the procedure.

Common sense sometimes isn't very common – but it can and should be.

A previous column included this comment. "Any positive quality (or decision or recommendation) when taken to an extreme becomes a negative."

That's precisely what happened that evening in that restaurant.

Looking at Something, and Then Seeing It

While on an extended road trip recently, I observed something that seemed to have a close relationship with business behavior. I realized driving activities offered some sound examples all of us can use in business. In the interest of full disclosure, my wife was driving while I was observing and thinking.

Here's what I saw: Drivers texting, talking on the phone, reading maps and newspapers, tuning radios, disciplining children, applying make-up, and a host of other things.

In addition to all that, many drivers also appeared to be connected to the steering wheel in a "death grip," staring hypnotically through the windshield looking neither left nor right. They were on their predetermined routes with no deviations or detours, traveling the course at a set speed (usually slower than the rest of the traffic).

These drivers were concentrating on a single task, moving from point A to point B with no distractions or variations – and no peripheral vision. They would probably get to their destinations, maybe a bit later than other drivers because of the slow pace, but chances were good that they'd get where they wanted to go.

I saw connections between what was happening on the road and what goes on in many businesses.

First, let's look at positive one. Without a doubt having a clear destination and route are as important in business as they are in taking a road trip. Without a clear end point, there is no way to set a course of action. Taking a trip requires knowing at least two reference points – where you start and where you want to go. Without knowing both points it's impossible to plot a course or know when to make corrections.

In business, having a goal is essential to allocating resources and assets. Knowing what you can use to start with will determine the difference between reality and wishful thinking. Without a plan it's impossible to quantify progress.

Now a negative. Fixing the focus on only what's directly out front – like staring through the windshield – eliminates knowing about other elements that could have an impact on the operator. That impact could be either literal as in a car, or figurative as in a business setting, but there will likely be consequences.

Traffic conditions change from minute to minute, and those changes require adjustments in speed and direction. Disregarding those changes can have serious repercussions. Likewise, missing the changing dynamics in business can have long lasting consequences.

When businesses and cars don't make the necessary course adjustments they usually cease to be safe or effective.

And what about those drivers who were dividing their attention between the requirements of safe driving and other distracting activities. They were "multitasking." Perhaps they believe they can do many things at the same time and do all of them well. Not so. I have a plaque on my office wall that aptly describes the implications of multi-tasking. It says, "Multi-tasking: Messing up everything simultaneously."

No matter how smart someone might be, it's impossible to devote one hundred percent attention to more than one item at a time. Something gets lost as soon as full attention shifts from one point to another. That shifting might be fast, but, by definition, attention has been redirected.

At the rate cars move and business climates shift, that momentary loss of attention could have long lasting implications. When drivers lose focus, vehicles drift from lane to lane. They slow down and speed up. The erratic activity makes it difficult to predict what movement might occur from moment to moment.

In business, false starts and unexpected reactions to changing conditions might likewise have significant consequences. No one can predict the future, but maintaining certain principles and practices can avoid serious accidents.

So, in the car and in the office, keep your eye on what's in front of you, but remember to watch both sides, and check in the rear view mirror, too.

You never know who or what might be overtaking you.

But What Does It Say?

Contrary to what many believe, the customer isn't always right – but he or she is always the customer – the person with the money. Exchanging money for goods or services is what business is all about. Pretty simple.

All it requires is a fair and equitable exchange. That, too, is simple until one party tries to get "the upper hand" and out maneuver the other.

Wonderful stories about the "good old days" describe when a handshake constituted a contract. We'll never know how true those stories were, but it seems in today's world we pay more attention to what someone might get away with that what someone will actually do.

"Truth" is stretched, and "Promises" are subject to interpretation. A formerly simple sentence like, "I'll do this," is now filled with qualifiers like: "I'll do this if, provided you, according to, when, under the condition that, et cetera…" That kind of wording results in confusing convoluted sentences.

"Clever" has replaced "Clear."

Television commercials are another interesting example of deception. For example: After making verbal statements about the benefits of a product, the print text says, "Results are not typical." If that's the case, what's the point of the commercial?

In addition, have you ever attempted to read the small print at the end of a commercial? Two problems are apparent with such text: it's too small, and one would have to be an accomplished "speed reader" to get through all the words.

Here's a broad generalization about print size and clarity. If the text is too small to read easily – beware. If something is difficult to read – read it!

When a writer wants someone to read his or her material he makes it easy to read. The author of difficult to read material didn't put it there to help the reader. He put it there to protect himself. In the event of a misunderstanding, that author can always say," It's right there." And it is – if you can find it.

The difference in attention is startling. Contract lawyers pour over every word and phrase, but many customers just look for the line where they sign their name. Bad idea!

And there is really no such thing as "boiler plate" in a contract. Every word has been carefully selected – to the advantage of the writer. In most instances, lawyers like to have "drafting rights" for preparing a contract. Although it entails work the "other side" doesn't have to do, authoring a contract allows the writer to include whatever he or she wants. It's then up to the other party to find the objectionable parts and get them removed.

So, when you have the opportunity, take the drafting rights, and do the initial writing. It could have a significant benefit.

The writing doesn't have to result in a long, complicated document. Sometimes only a few lines in a Letter of Agreement can avoid future complications and hard feelings.

Years ago, I authored a book with a colleague, John. Our simple Letter of Agreement stated we would share equally all the writing and then share equally whatever benefits we derived.

We signed and dated the letter and put it away.

As we neared completion, John told me his wife had commented she thought he was contributing more to the process than I was. She felt he should be entitled to more than half of any future royalties. Potential Problem! She was mistaken, but had it been so, such a late date restructure would have had a serious impact on our writing project.

The danger abated quickly when I opened my briefcase, took out the Letter, showed it to him, and said, "Remember this?" End of discussion.

We completed the book. It was published, and we happily shared the royalties equally for a long time.

I would not presume to offer these examples as legal advice. They're just reminders of how important it is to pay attention to what we see and sign.

Remember, "Caveat emptor." That's always good advice.

No One Can See You

In 1897, HG Wells wrote a chilling story about Dr. Jack Griffin, a researcher who discovered a drug that would make him invisible. He also made two subsequent discoveries. He couldn't reverse the process to become visible again, and the side effects of the drug drove him insane.

The book was made into a motion picture in 1933, starring Claude Rains, and it became a classic horror movie. In 2008, *The Invisible Man* was selected for preservation in the United States National Film Registry by the Library of Congress as being, "culturally, historically, and aesthetically significant."

"Monocane," the drug central to the story line, doesn't exist, of course, but widespread behavior in business, government, religion, and society in general often demonstrates the same result.

Sometimes, real people become invisible! Although we can still see them physically, they become unimportant or meaningless.

One of the easiest and best examples of invisibility is demonstrated when someone stands at a Customer Service counter. (By the way – that's often an oxymoron.) All too often, the clerk is occupied with activities that render a customer invisible. No eye contact. No service. It's as if the customer doesn't exist.

The ignored customer might just as well be living in another dimension. That lack of awareness infuriates customers, but there is another side to the story. We've all seen those same angry customers then exit the store or office and walk right past someone raising money for charity selling candy or ringing a bell next to a red kettle! Invisibility works both ways.

So when encountering other people, acknowledge them. Look them in the eye. When we make them visible we become visible, too.

On another, perhaps more serious note, it seems many people today are more reluctant to take stands on issues or voice opinions than they were in the past. They are more inclined to remain invisible and let others make decisions for them rather than standing up and speaking up on what they consider to be important issues.

They don't want to "make waves" by disagreeing, but rather to "go along to get along."

Here's the problem with such behavior. Being invisible by saying nothing or doing nothing doesn't mean one is not participating in an activity. Inaction and invisibility provide support for an opponent or an opposing belief.

Business pressures created by new laws, rules, and regulations are increasing daily to the point it's difficult to make plans. Education, civic, and governmental changes also require attention and active participation in order to maintain stability.

The interesting paradox here is the fact that everyone – even the silent one - has a position on everything. People like or dislike, agree or disagree about everyday issues large and small. All too often, however, they keep that position private, and they justify the silence by saying, "What difference does it make what I think? I'm just one person."

What individuals think makes a huge difference! But it's necessary to communicate those otherwise private thoughts because we don't live in a society of mind readers.

Whenever groups or individuals remain mute – or invisible – on issues, they give up the right to complain if they disagree with the ultimate decision.

If anyone abstains from a vote, for example, the abstention is the same as voting for and aiding the prevailing side. It allows others to decide for the inactive individual.

Many people think they are being "neutral," but they aren't. Remember the old adage, "Action speaks louder than words?" So does inaction!

When someone elects to become invisible by not standing up, speaking up, or showing up; he or she is giving up. Every voice and every action, overt or covert, contributes to the ultimate decision.

In many respects, no one can remain neutral. Everyone is either for or against an idea. And it's important to be able to see and identify the stance.

So, if you're wearing a "cloak of invisibility," take it off. Be seen and heard so others don't speak for you.

Action – Reaction – Consequence

A recent newscast provided an example of sensitive and brave behavior by a corporate employee as well as the implications, reactions, and consequences of his action.

The story recounted what a restaurant waiter did, why he did it, and what happened as a result of his actions.

To set the scene, this waiter, let's call him "Sam," chose to act because, in his own words, "It was the right thing to do." A wonderful model for all of us!

Here's what happened. A young child with Down Syndrome was dining with his parents in a local restaurant when Sam became aware of another patron ridiculing the little boy by making fun of the child's behavior. Sam told the patron to stop, and he refused to wait on the offending customer and his party.

Now, this was risky because his job was to wait on tables not to be an advocate for another customer – regardless of the reason. But, at personal risk, Sam confronted the man.

How many of us would have done that?

Sam could have ignored the offending customer, or gone about his business, and let the little boy's parents handle the situation if they so desired. Sam could have thought, "Not my problem."

Choices for all the parties were clear: the parents could ignore the insults, leave the restaurant, or confront the clod.

The people with the offending customer could correct him, ignore him, or laugh along with him and encourage him.

Other patrons who witnessed the actions did nothing. Only one person acted to stop the insulting and insensitive behavior – Sam.

He risked his job.

Here's the next reaction. When the rude and thoughtless customer reacted loudly to Sam's comments, the restaurant owner, Sam's boss, appeared. The customer complained, again loudly, about how Sam had treated him.

Now, the owner had to make a decision. Should he support the customer because, "the customer is always right," or should he support his employee?

When he learned the details of the incident, the owner backed Sam! He agreed Sam had done the right thing, and the customer had been out of line. When the customer became even angrier and louder, the manager suggested to the customer that it would be best for everyone if he and his party would leave the restaurant.

The next reaction came from the community. With the number of ever-present cell phones and video recorders, it wasn't long before the incident became a topic on local news and social media outlets.

The overwhelming response from the local community was positive, and business at the restaurant increased. "Regulars" returned in large numbers to support the restaurant and what Sam and the owner had done for the little boy and his family.

New customers came in droves because they had seen the story in print and in the electronic media. They wanted to offer their support for taking the position and to offer a clear "Well Done" to everyone involved.

The take-away from this series of events is this. A "chain reaction" always follows actions and decisions. Because things don't occur in isolation, we should be mindful of what we do and be prepared to accept the impact of the "ripple effect" that follows a decision. Sometimes that ripple is obvious and immediate, and other times it is subtle and delayed.

I have used a motto many times in past columns, and it's appropriate here as we look at action, reaction, and consequences. Here's the motto: Whatever you do, do it on purpose.

That way, business realities as well as our individual beliefs, core values, and ethics will drive and justify how we act toward customers, clients, colleagues, and, of course, family members.

Sam's action in that restaurant took on a life of its own.

His actions could have resulted in him being on the unemployment line or the morning television talk programs.

He didn't care about that. He did "what was right."

What a lesson for all of us!

Gifts to Give and Receive

Everyone knows it's more difficult, and more expensive, to get a new customer than it is to keep an existing one. Yet we often take our existing customers for granted. They have kept us in business, but we tend to ignore them when we offer promotions.

Frequently, we see invitations to "Open a new charge card and receive a discount on all your purchases today," but existing charge card holders pay full price for everything!

It might be advantageous for a customer to close an existing account and open a new one at a competing establishment. I know opening and closing charge accounts would raise havoc with credit scores, and I'm certainly not suggesting anyone do that, but it's interesting, isn't it?

My simple question is this. What message does a business send when it ignores existing customers in favor of potential new customers? Wouldn't it be thoughtful to recognize and reward long-term and loyal customers the same way we entice new customers?

If you currently hold a charge card, some companies offer promotions indicating, "If you spend X dollars today, you'll receive a Y percent discount." But the new customers get the discount without a minimum purchase.

I have a charge card that I received from a major department store decades ago. (Long before many of their current employees were born.) I have never received anything that indicated, "Because you're such a good, long-time customer, enjoy an X percent discount on your purchases today."

Wouldn't that be a positive example of good customer service?

What I'm suggesting is that we "Consider Our Customers" – All of them – All the time.

A current television commercial provides this interesting example. The owner of a florist store apologizes to a customer because her computer is running so slowly. Turns out the customer knows about available software (Made by the sponsor of the commercial), and he installs it free of charge.

Instantly, her computer is running like new.

After thanking him, she says, "And the flowers are on the house."

The customer didn't "do a deal" to get something for nothing. He did it to help. There was no quid pro quo.

The owner showed her gratitude by giving him a gift.

There are many gifts we can give our customers, and it's appropriate to think about them particularly at this time of year.

So, once again, "Consider Our Customers" by giving simple gifts like these:

Attention: Look at them when you talk to them, and look at them when they talk to you. Eye contact is essential in this part of the world if we want to develop positive relationships with customers. That relationship should be more than exchanging money.

Assistance: When customers ask for help locating an item, resist the temptation to simply say, "It's over there" or "Down that aisle." Escort the customer to the item. It takes a few moments, of course, but the gesture will be remembered long after the customer leaves. And, that customer will likely describe the action to friends and colleagues. Great advising at no cost.

Consideration: A customer comes with a need, a problem, or a requirement; and we can help. We know more about what we can offer than the customer does, so take the time to ask questions. Identify the product or service that will help. Sometimes customers don't know precisely what they want to ask for because the requirement or situation might be new to them.

Because of what we know, we can be instant problem-solvers for customers when we take the time to work with them.

Time: Time is a precious and personal commodity. When we give of our time, we give of ourselves; and customers will remember how we made them feel when they came to our place of business.

There are no price tags on any of these gifts, but there is plenty of payback, and that's good for everyone.

To Lie or Not to Lie – That is the Question

Let's begin with a few questions about events that come up often, and require all of us to react. Here they are.

If a supplier reduces the content of a box but not the size of the box and charges the same price, is he telling a lie?

If a bottler converts from quarts to liters but maintains the same price per bottle, is he telling a lie?

If an insurance company eliminates specific coverage but maintains the same premium price, is that a lie?

When an automobile company promises specific fuel economy but then qualifies the number by using selected variables, is that a lie?

Are these intentional deceptions, or are they just examples of the old "caveat emptor" warning? Must the "buyer beware" because the seller has a right to be deceptive?

What happened to the old "Golden Rule" of treating others as you want to be treated?

What happened to the basic principle of honesty? Telling the truth because it's the right thing to do?

The concept is obvious everywhere:

Thou shalt not bear false witness.

A Scout is Trustworthy.

It's a sin to tell a lie, as Fats Waller wrote in his 1969 song.

Tell the truth, the whole truth, and nothing but the truth.

Recently, that precept seems to have changed with the US Supreme Court's announcement that it is perfectly acceptable to lie about military service and decorations for valor. The court said it is okay to lie in select situations. That causes many interpretation problems. A lie was once unacceptable, but now it might be fine, and lies are even protected under the First Amendment.

It's certainly confusing, and I'm reminded of the wonderful lyrics Oscar Hammerstein II wrote for *The King And I* when he had the king sing, "A Puzzlement" which includes these words:

When I was a boy, the world was better spot.
What was so was so, what was not was not.
Now I am a man, the world has changed a lot
Some things nearly so, others nearly not.

There are times I almost think
I am not sure of what I absolutely know.
Very often find confusion
In conclusion I concluded long ago.

Our worlds now, business, social, and civic have become a "puzzlement." If it's okay to lie to stay out of trouble like the self-proclaimed (but false) Medal of Honor recipient, what about providing false information on a credit application? What about taking an oath in court and then not telling the truth? How about falsifying a business contract to obtain improved financial terms? And what about the proverbial question of shouting, "Fire" in a crowded theater?

Here is another example of telling untruths, but this time without negative intent. Recently, I re-read a book which upset the advertising world when it was published in 1957. We're seeing a revisiting of much of what was described then as we look at market research and polling data predicting how people will behave. In *The Hidden Persuaders*, Vance Packard said, "…what people tell interviewers had only a remote bearing on how they might actually behave."

Market researchers described three basic findings.

First, "You can't assume that people know what they want."

Second, "You can't assume people will tell you the truth about their wants and dislikes even if they know them."

And third, "It is dangerous to assume that people can be trusted to behave in a rational way."

As we continue to develop products, services, and relationships, keeping a close eye on our basic core values seems essential to help us navigate the confusing conditions and options we face every day. Although the specific conditions might change, the core values don't. Staying true to those values might be difficult sometimes, but back-tracking is even more difficult and costly.

Those values will help us avoid the puzzlements of business. Those values will enable us to stand by the conclusions we concluded long ago.

CHAPTER 4

Selling Skills

An interesting survey was done years ago in which salespeople and buyers were asked this question: "What bothers you most about salespeople?"

The vast majority of buyers said, "They talk too much."

Surprisingly, the majority of salespeople said, "We talk too much."

Why would salespeople do that when they know they're not helping themselves?

A productive way to stop such behavior is this:

Ask questions, and then listen to the answers.

A sales interaction should not be about "Selling." It should be about "Buying."

And the best way to encourage that is to ask a customer what he or she wants or needs.

Offer that, and you'll likely make a sale.

You may be the greatest pen salesperson in the world, but if you don't find out the customer needs something he or she can easily erase you will never sell your pens.

Using Language to Deceive

The language used when describing products and services often doesn't really mean what it says, making it increasingly difficult to separate truth from fiction in many business situations.

Fast talking television commercials hawk products that are "not available in stores," but can be found everywhere – drug stores, hardware stores, notions stores, etc. Why are viewers subjected to the deception?

Whatever happened to the concept of "truth in advertising?"

The general public experiences these distortions with such frequency it's easy to see why they become jaded.

But wait. There's more!

A walk through any supermarket provides ample evidence of deception. Look at packaging. In many instances, the size and price of a package remain the same, but the contents of that package have been diminished.

That's a price increase without notice. The intention of the packager – not the store management – is to make the customer think the value of his or her purchase has remained stable when it hasn't.

As a side bar, let me once again suggest reading an interesting and probing book about the subject of deception in marketing. Vance Packard's *The Hidden Persuaders* was originally published in 1957, and revised in 1980. A more contemporary edition, authored by Mark Crispin Miller, was released in 2007. Many of the specific examples used in the early versions are now outdated, of course, but the basic principles detailed in the book still apply today.

You won't have to start on page one and navigate through to the end.

Just open it anywhere, begin reading, and you'll find stark examples of deception through language.

It's an easy read; it's enlightening; and, in parts, it's frightening.

Now back to our immediate concern.

Air travel provides an appropriate illustration of language use because it's interesting to observe just how often some airlines "stretch the truth" about services and performance.

For example, as I'm writing this, I'm sitting in an airline waiting area. All the high tech communication technology throughout the airport is announcing an "on time" departure, but my plane, which should have departed an hour ago, has not yet arrived!

In the "old days," airline personnel would make updates with printed cards slipped into frames behind the agent's location. That was time-consuming and reason for lack of updates, but today a few keystrokes on a computer can update every screen throughout an entire airport.

So, why do some airlines continue to provide incorrect information?

At the moment, there is another example of language deception having a significant impact on all of us. It relates to how government budgets are described. There is no question the budgets of governments and their various agencies are far more complex than personal budgets, but most people understand the basics of a budget.

Money comes in, and we calculate what we can spend based on that income. When we get a raise we can spend more because we have more.

A raise is a raise. More is more, and less is less. Sounds obvious, but here's where the language of government becomes deceptive.

In government budgets, when an increase isn't as large as someone projects, the new amount is called a reduction even though it is still larger than the original amount.

Here's an example. Think of a government agency with an operating budget of $10,000. Obviously, no such agency exists, but this will work for illustrative purposes. When the agency projects an increase to $11,000, but receives only $10,500, that is described as a reduction. The result is identified as a budget cut even though there is $500 more in the budget – $500 more to spend.

Talk about "voodoo math" and deceptive use of language!

In government budgets, more is often described as less.

Because language can be deceiving, it's important for all of us in business to be aware of how some deceivers manipulate language, our perceptions, and ultimately, our actions.

To modify a popular phrase: "Be aware – be very aware."

Sending is Just the Start

On the surface, the communication process is pretty simple. Somebody (a "sender") sends a message to somebody else (a "receiver"). When that person gets the message, he or she interprets it and responds to the original sender. That's it!

But the process deserves deeper attention or the result isn't communication. It's transmission. Every one of us, in our business and personal situations, must pay attention to the details of the process, or it will fail. Let's look at how we might stumble.

The role of the "sender" is to construct the message in a way appropriate for the ultimate receiver – not for the sender's personal convenience. In business we assume the sender knows something about the receiver.

Most of today's commonplace phone technology enables a caller to leave a recorded message if the called party doesn't answer. That's no surprise to anyone today because leaving a "voice mail" message is common practice.

The problem revolves around the behavior of the caller. In many instances, the caller decides the end of the communication process. It shouldn't be!

Many callers believe it is sufficient to think, "I left a message. My job is finished."

But communication doesn't happen until the called party receives the message. Without reception, the call is just one-way transmission.

Many companies engage staff to place such calls to inform or remind people of appointments or deliveries.

Once the call is made, though, they move down their call list and make other calls – never returning to the unanswered call.

And that's the heart of the matter – considering the receiver.

Placing a call is fine, but if it isn't received, for all intents and purposes, it didn't happen. Sometimes such a call is followed by another call or an email with this message, "If you didn't get my phone call, please let me know." How in the world could anyone respond to that if there was no knowledge of the first message?

This also happens with unanswered emails when the sender delivers a second message stating, "If you didn't receive this, let me know, and I'll send it again.

Just leaving such a message on a phone or on a computer can be compared to putting a note into a bottle and throwing it into the ocean. It's being sent, but there is no assurance it will ever be received.

That is an exaggeration, of course, but it makes the point that "sending" a message is not enough. Obviously to be of value, it must be received.

Here is an example of sending a message with good intentions but with no concept of the need to "close the communication loop" by addressing the needs of the receiver. It's hard to believe this story is true, but it is.

A business executive had flown from San Francisco to New York for a meeting. When he checked into the hotel he told the desk clerk he needed a strong wake-up call because he had a hearing impairment. "Of course, sir." replied the clerk, and made a note of the call-time.

The next morning the unexpected sunlight awakened the executive before the wake-up call came. He was three time zones away from home and the morning light was quite different. As he dressed, he thought, "This is a nice way to start the day. Early." Then he noticed a piece of paper had been slipped under the door. Thinking it was his bill he read it and was jolted by surprising news.

It wasn't the bill but a note from the desk clerk. It read, "This is your wake-up call, sir. We know you have a hearing impairment, but you can obviously read so we were sure this would get you started on time. Have a good day."

When he looked at his watch he discovered he had overslept and was already an hour and a half late for his meeting!

The clerk's intentions were good, but the execution was terrible.

Effective communication is always about the receiver!

Respect vs. Presumption

It seems that more and more businesses are working hard at being "chummy" with customers, and in doing so, they become presumptuous.

In all kinds of contacts – telephone, email, letters, and face-to-face – business people are attempting to be friends with every customer, or potential customer.

It's worth considering the fact that, although some customers might be friends, prospective customers are not our friends. We don't even know them!

Yet we often presume to address them by their first names rather than to show them the respect they deserve. It's just common courtesy to address strangers by their sir names not by their given names.

Aside from being presumptuous, using a first name when reading the script on a prospecting call is a dead giveaway that a "sales call" has arrived. Here's a personal example. When I answer the phone and the caller says, "Hello, John,. How are you today?" I drop any interest in continuing the conversation. Although my first name is "John" I always use my middle name, "Robert." When the first name is used, I know the caller doesn't know me even though he or she has presumed to use my first name.

Even more foolish, emails are often addressed this way, "Hi, J," or "Dear J," or simply "J."

How chummy is that?

One simple word describes good customer service – Respect.

Respect the person. Respect the current customers, Respect the potential customers.

The advent of the computer and the ability to acquire and develop huge mailing lists make a sham out of personal customer service.

A generic message is programmed into the computer – and everyone gets the same "personal" letter. No one believes such letters are designed specifically for the recipient, but, strangely, many business operators believe that's a good way to do business.

Just throw out as many "personal" letters as you can, and some of them will produce a positive result. Some do, but what's missed with this approach is the fact that all those non-impressed recipients are alienated by the bothersome mail, emails, and phone calls.

Intruding on and wasting someone's time is no way to acquire a new customer, and showing disrespect makes absolutely no sense in any business or personal relationship.

An old adage about effective communication states, "It's all about the audience – in this case, the customer."

And respecting the individual should be of paramount importance to any businessperson.

All too often these days, speed takes precedence over attention. Get a message out as quickly as possible to as many people as possible, and play the percentages. Such instant messages are fast, but often they are also inaccurate.

Also, they focus on what the businessperson wants to tell rather than what might be important to the targeted potential customer.

Years ago, Tom Peters summed up customer service in this single sentence. "Find out what the customer wants and give it to him." The legendary retail department store owner, Marshall Field predated him by generations when he said, "Give the lady what she wants."

What potential customers certainly don't want from a business is interruptive phone calls or "friendly and chummy" letters taking personal liberties about an assumed relationship.

So, all of us in business would be well advised to ask ourselves these simple questions when we're reaching out to prospective customers: "What would potential customers like from me? What do they expect from me?"

We know what we want from them, but if we don't concentrate on their needs, expectations, and desires we are taking chances about sending inappropriate messages.

Many marketers today follow a regimen that states, "If you throw enough stuff at enough people often enough some of it might stick."

Playing the odds like that is risky – and it's also expensive.

Demonstrating respect, on the other hand, is safe and cost-effective.

Samuel Goldwin said, "Once you learn to fake sincerity, you've got it made." That sounds crass, but being respectful to potential customers (even if you don't want to) will likely produce better results than the alternative.

Delicate Balance

Providing a product or service in any business enterprise is a constantly changing series of events that require attention and adjustments.

If an operator assumes that money will always come in, chances are good that the business won't last very long.

The cash flow and the customers are always changing. It's doubtful that anyone has ever seen a financial statement where the income line is smooth. There are always ups and downs. It's the trend that is important just as it is in any personal household budget. Some days and weeks are better than others; the important element is the picture at the end of the year.

In order to maintain the positive trend, business operators constantly look for ways to balance the pressing elements, but sometimes that balance is pushed too far. Here's an example.

Telephone inquiries to a business are often answered with a robo voice informing the caller the call is being recorded "for security" or "for training purposes." Sounds good, and sounds as if the company is doing the caller a favor. But that isn't necessarily true.

Such calls are often used for training, but there are no assurances about who is being – or might be – trained some time in the future. There is no mention of how the training will be presented either. Further, there are no assurances the recorded information will actually remain secure. Certainly, using actual customer calls can be valuable, but those recordings are often duplicated and distributed to other corporate locations. With turnover and attrition it's quite possible "unauthorized" trainees will leave the company – with secure information including credit card numbers, Social Security numbers, and birth dates. Perfect material for identity theft. The desire to provide good customer service must be balanced with appreciation and concern for customer security.

Leaving recorded information is about as secure as posting it on a supermarket bulletin board with a notice, "Do Not Read."

During a call I made recently, when I declined to provide my SS number, the company representative said, "Well then, there isn't anything we can do for you." And she disconnected me. My guess is corporate wouldn't be happy with the treatment, but she was doing her job as she thought she was instructed to do it.

All too often, there is a disconnect between the actions of the customer service department and providing service to a customer. That operator wasn't providing much service.

A CEO once told me something interesting about his company focus and a change that was made as a result of an observation. He said, "We were so focused on the bottom line we forgot about our customers."

There is no question about the importance of the bottom line and the continuing existence of a company. But if the customer doesn't receive proper attention, that, too will have a severe impact on the financial picture of a company.

We are so focused on our own activities that we often forget this simple fact.

No matter what product or service we offer, someone else offers essentially that same product or service.

Another fact we sometimes overlook, although we know it well, is the fact it is easier and cheaper to keep an existing customer than it is to acquire a new one. And customers talk!

Sometimes they talk long and loud, and dissatisfied customers talk longer and louder than satisfied ones. And they talk to more people than do the ones that are pleased with the product or service.

One more obvious, but sometimes overlooked, element related to customer service. It's important to remember the interaction is a conversation between the two parties both of whom are strangers to each other and will likely never speak again.

So customer service representatives should never assume a close or informal relationship is appropriate. Formal, respectful methods of address are expected in business. Don't presume to call someone by his or her first name. Use Mr., Mrs., Ms., or Miss.

AND never use "Dear," "Honey," or "Sweetheart!"

CHAPTER 5

Interviewing

Interviews are a fact of life we all face from time to time. We're interviewed for a job, to get into a school, to get a promotion, to serve as a witness, to be on a radio or television program, even to become Miss America.

Most of us are uncomfortable because we don't know what we'll be asked.

The following essays offer advice, but here's something to remember every time you are interviewed – for any reason.

You know more about yourself than anyone else does, so you'll be able to talk about t yourself better than anyone else can.

Think of an interview as a conversation –not as an interrogation. In a conversation you offer opinions, ask questions, and choose to agree or disagree with the other participant.

That's precisely how to approach an interview. You're not "on the spot." You're an equal partner in a conversation.

The following pages will provide examples and support, but, once again, remember you know more about yourself than anyone else does, so take the interview opportunity to share your information.

Ask the "Right" Question

Recently, I had the radio turned on, and, although I wasn't fully tuned in to the talk program, I remember a comment the guest made because it provided such a strong message for anyone in business.

He said: "Ask the wrong question, and you'll get the wrong answer."

No one deliberately seeks a wrong answer, but without sufficient forethought that's exactly what can result. This is particularly significant during live interviews – whether you're conducting the interview or someone else is interviewing you.

Here's an example. If you're conducting an interview to identify how a potential employee might fit into your organization, avoid setting the direction of the answer by asking the prospect to identify his or her "biggest weaknesses."

That request yields a litany of weaknesses.

On the other hand if you ask the applicant about his or her "greatest strengths" you'll get a litany of strengths.

In both instances, you'll get precisely what you asked for – a litany. That wasn't your intent – but you told the other person what to include.

So let's review some of the basic techniques for asking questions in order to assure you'll get what you need.

First, when you want to gather as much information as possible, ask the "Open" questions that begin with the words, "How," "Why," "What." (*How* do you propose to continue working and finishing your degree at the same time? *Why* is this a good time for a job change? *What* do you think an MBA degree will do for you?)

Those questions require extensive thought and cannot be completed with just a word or two.

Such questions allow the respondent to indicate what is of interest and importance to him or her. In other words, the questioner will pick the playing field location, but the respondent will select the game.

The questioner doesn't set any boundaries when he or she keeps the questions very broad.

Another example: Asking, "What is your favorite pastime?" will yield much more information about the respondent than asking, "What is your favorite movie?" The response to the second question will be the title of a motion picture, but the response to the first question could be anything from watching movies, to SCUBA diving, or other activities about which the questioner is totally unaware.

Following up that response with, "Why?" or "Tell me more about that" will advance the conversation by providing broad, possibly unexpected, information.

Using open questions will collect a lot of data, but sooner or later you'll have to get specific. Narrow the discussion by using Closed questions that begin with the words, "Who," "When, "Where," "How many."

These allow the questioner to select the topics, and the responder simply plugs in the data. Closed questions can be answered in just a few words, but use them carefully.

If closed questions come too quickly the interview might begin to feel like an interrogation rather than a conversation.

Interrogations produce defense mechanisms. Stay with conversation.

When you go for the specific data here's a way to get the information without creating pressure. Use a "Conditional Question" which begins with the word "If." It works like this:

"*If* you are the successful candidate, when *might* you be able to start? That will give you the information you want about a date, but the respondent still has some latitude.

Now, here's a useful tactic when you're the one being interviewed. To make your point feel free to turn closed questions into open ones or vice versa. Like this.

A closed question asking, "Who will run the project?" can be rephrased to this open question. "How are we going to select the project manager?"

Likewise, an open question like, "How are you going to select the project manager?" can be rephrased to, "Who will run the project?

Be sure to stay with the issue when you rephrase, or you might be seen as evasive, and that's never good for business.

So, ask the RIGHT question, and you'll get the right answer.

Doesn't that make sense?

Who Says What? – Why?

This book is release in early May, and depending upon one's perspective, that can be "the best of times," or it can be "the worst of times." Thanks to Charles Dickens and the first sentence of *A Tale of Two Cities*.

Summer is almost here, the school year is almost over, and vacations are just around the corner. That's just some of the "best." But what about the "worst?" For many that could be job hunting – either a part-time summer job, or it could be the start of a career after graduation. Either way it can be daunting for the job seeker.

But it can also be difficult for the person charged with the responsibility of hiring an applicant. That selection process usually concludes with a personal interview after application forms have been submitted.

Let's look at the interview and consider the roles the parties play – the Interviewer and the Applicant.

In every such situation, two agendas are evident.

From all the applicants, the Interviewer has to select the one person best suited for the position. The Applicant, on the other hand, must win out over all the other interested parties. This is a true competition with a single winner and lots of losers. What behaviors can be significant for each party to display during this interaction?

First, when you are the Interviewer. Whether a large corporation or a small local business, this role is to select the one person who will best represent the business, be willing to learn the specifics of the business, and relate well to customers and co-workers. The selection is often described as this three-step process: Can *do – Will Do – Fit.*

Information on the ability and experience of an applicant is easy to find in an application form before scheduling an interview, and be sure to read the form before the interview! Use your skills and experience to learn about the person behind the form.

Respect the Applicant. This person is nervous so help him or her have a positive experience. In that sense, be a teacher as well as an interviewer.

Now, the Applicant. What can you do to be successful during an interview? First of all, remember this simple and obvious fact. You know more about yourself than the interviewer does.

During the interview, your responsibility is to convince someone else of your potential value to the company and why you should be hired. It's like selling a product. If you were a pen salesperson you would talk about everything you know about your product – what it can do, where it was made, what it's made of, what it costs, why it's better than the competition, etc., etc., etc.

Do the same thing about yourself. Don't wait for the interviewer to ask a question about something you know and would like to discuss. The interviewer doesn't know as much as you do – so speak up. If the information is new and interesting you'll hear the interviewer say, "Tell me more about that."

Now, you are participating in a conversation – and not responding to an interrogation. Always remember that an interview is a conversation, and both parties can contribute to the content. As with the pen salesman example, remember to "Ask for the sale." Be sure to indicate clearly that you want to work at the company (if that's true) and what you can bring to the position.

Don't assume the Interviewer will figure that out. That's not the interviewer's responsibility; that's yours.

Finally, be aware of the impression you make by how you present yourself. First impressions are important, powerful, and permanent. Here are a few reminders about behaviors often overlooked during the pressure of preparing for and participating in a job interview.

Look at the interviewer. Sounds obvious, but all too often, it doesn't happen. Talk to the person, not to the desktop. Talk loudly enough to be easily heard. Also, when you increase your volume, your voice will be rich and full, and you'll appear confidant and assured – even if you aren't.

Finally, start preparing for those interviews by being careful with entries on the "social media." Interviewers often check those entries looking for the "Did do," along with the "Can do."

What might be funny on a computer could be disastrous in an interview.

Apply these skills, and at the conclusion of your interview you'll be able to quote the last line in *A Tale Of Two Cities*.

"It is a far, far better thing that I do than I have ever done…"

What If…

If Wilbur and Orville had known in 1903 what we know now, would they have built that funny looking airplane rather than a Boeing 747?

If Henry Ford knew in 1908 what we know now would he have built the Model T or a Lamborghini Aventador?

Those are both rather silly questions because the developments that took place during the passing century produced information and created opportunities inconceivable one hundred years ago.

Playing such "mind games" might be fun, but there is no way such questions can be answered with any accuracy and they produce no valuable information.

So why do we hear them so often from reporters and other news-gatherers? Easy. They create the impression of deep thought and probing pursuits. In reality, though, they provide little more than the chance to ask more questions and create a biased perspective.

We're being exposed to such hypothetical questions now with increasing frequency as we move forward on the political campaign trail. Many reporters who use the hypothetical question techniques seem to be more interested in creating a story than they are in reporting events.

On the business front, some "creative" HR department personnel are now asking such questions too as part of the formal hiring interviews. In such situations, there is more of a focus on creativity than on accuracy. Such interviewers look for the creative answers they like, agree with, or find interesting rather than answers that are correct – or wrong.

It's a guessing game about the intent of the interviewer when he or she asks a question like this: "If you were invisible, what would you do this evening?" Where can you go with that?

Here's a way to respond to hypothetical questions in any arena including the board room, the TV or radio studio, when looking for a job, or in a selling situation to name just a few.

Don't answer a hypothetical question!

Good reporters and good business interviewers respect a response like, "That's an interesting question, but no one can really answer a hypothetical question. However, what I can tell you is…" Then open a topic that is relevant to the issue, the position, the company, or about yourself.

When you bring up an interesting fact in such a context, the interviewer is likely to follow up on your answer and ask for more information. In that way, you are truly contributing to a conversation and not just trying to think up "cleaver" responses to unexpected questions.

If you were applying for an acting position with an improvisational theater organization, those clever lines would probably work to your advantage but not necessarily so in the business or political worlds.

As with a presentation, in an interview the focus should be the audience, and every presentation is for the benefit of the audience. In an HR setting the interviewer is the audience so focus and relate your remarks toward the business areas and the specific company that's interested in learning about you.

In a television or radio interview, the host or reporter is merely a conduit. Your "ultimate audience," the one you want to inform or convince, is the viewer or the listener.

The setting for the interview is merely a vehicle through which to reach the true audience.

If during any type of interview, you get surprised and knocked off track, take a deep breath, pause, and bridge back to the point or points you want to make. Use bridging statements like: "That's why it's important for us to talk about…" "Let me expand on the comment I made a moment ago." "If we take a step back we can better see where this line of questions is going." "Let me see if I understand this. You want to…"

Always remember an interview, like a presentation is a conversation. It's not an interrogation. Both parties have an equal right to contribute.

And, if you ever feel you're getting into trouble, remember these words of wisdom.

"When you realize you're digging yourself into a hole –stop digging."

Simple – Obvious – Brilliant.

Two Sides Of The Same Coin

The choices we make in an instant – good or bad – can live with us forever. A recent news item demonstrated what technology can do for us or to us – both good and bad. Just in case some readers might have missed the news piece, here is a brief review.

A young woman, self-described as drunk, recorded herself on video as she was driving home in her car while under the influence of alcohol. She was using a new technology (Periscope) to record and transmit her "adventure."

She was found and arrested for DUI as a result of using that video device.

A police office in the area saw the live streaming, recognized some of the landmarks she was passing, tracked her down, and stopped her. After administering a field sobriety test, he arrested her. That arrest and that DUI will remain part of her driving record.

Fortunately, she didn't injure herself or anyone else during this "joy ride."

Obviously, alcohol impaired her judgment in doing something this foolish – and dangerous. It might have seemed like a "good idea" to her when she got behind the wheel of her car. She likely planned to impress or entertain friends, but at what risk?

That drive was a short-term activity with long-term consequences for her.

Most people wouldn't consider doing such a thing, but the increasing presence and availability of this type of technology in a variety of situations, if used carelessly, can cause unexpected problems long after an activity.

Here's a simple bit of advice related to this new technology as well as others yet to be invented.

Never, never, never record or stream anything you wouldn't want your family, friends, classmates, clergy, teachers, spouse, children, employers – or potential employers – to see now, next year, or ever.

There are no exceptions to that advice!

Producing the video is easy; living with the unintended consequences might be devastating, painful, and it will be permanent.

Because of the ease of recording, many employers are now using this technology as the first cut in the hiring process by conducting remote interviews. College admissions officers include it as a selection criterion. And even "bad guys" find it helpful when looking for victims.

It's easy to select what we put into communication systems, but we can't control everywhere it goes or everyone who might receive it. And that's a serious problem.

On the other hand, this medium is an excellent way to promote and introduce yourself to the world. By using care and discretion it can demonstrate talents, accomplishments, and skills. It can assist engaging others and show who you are and what you can do.

It can serve as an "Open Sesame" for developing contacts, opportunities, and careers. However, remember that something simple can also be extremely dangerous.

When simple things get out of control, often they can't be stopped. An example: It's easier to put out a campfire than a forest fire!

Activities that seem to be humorous at the start (like that foolish "joy ride") can present a completely different picture later in life when seeking employment or academic recognition. Once those messages are sent, they live forever.

We can't see all the people who view the recordings, but they can see us.

It's in our best interest, both professionally and personally, to explore and master the new technologies as they come on the scene. That takes a little work and study, but the results can be life changing.

Most people today find it difficult to even consider having to go through their daily activities without a cell phone and a computer. Not long ago, we all did it because we had no other option. Now it is almost unthinkable!

But, whatever technology and behavioral choices you make, make them on purpose and recognize the implications and the potential impact.

Ask yourself this simple question, "Will I be embarrassed or ashamed if someone important to me sees this recording tomorrow, next week, or next year?"

Let your answer guide your choice.

CHAPTER 6

Technology

Advances in technology allow us to do things in new and different ways. Some of it even allows us to do things" never before possible.

Whatever the case, however, it's important to remember why we're using it. It's to accomplish something – to use a tool or a technique to make an improvement.

It isn't – or shouldn't be – just for the sake of doing something a different way. It isn't – or shouldn't – be to "play with a new toy just because we can.

The appearance of new technology seems to trigger a desire in some people to just accept a new technique rather than to make improvements.

These new tools appear on the horizon wirh great rapidity, and if we're not careful those new tools can cause conflict and problems.

By all means, use the new technology- just be careful not to be used by it – or by those touting its merits simply to sell more of it.

Don't Fall In Love Too Easily

Seventy years ago, a plaintive song proclaimed, "I Fall In Love Too Easily" (Music by Julie Styne, Lyrics by Sammy Cahn). It had a soothing melody and pleasant lyrics, but the message foreshadowed potential problems in the motion picture, *Anchors Aweigh*.

The emotional attachment and potential long-term relationships were tempered by two simple words – "too easily."

In many respects our work place and personal interactions with technology are similar to the message of the song. New "things" come to the market. Many customers "fall in love" with them. The rapid rates of change and "improvements" have contributed to our current disposable society. Although that's good for business, all too often some of the personal decisions and choices are made more because of the "new" than because of the "need."

Not long ago when a person was asked how many computers he or she had the answer came quickly. "None" or maybe "One." Today, the question usually requires a couple of moments of thought before a number is offered. Computers are everywhere. On the desk, in the briefcase, even on the wrist.

Now, what does "falling in love" have to do with business and instructional hardware? Often the advent of a new device results in discarding previous devices and practices in favor of the new "toy" – because it's new.

A while ago I told the story of a participant in a corporate seminar session asking if he could use his new tablet to deliver his presentation. I said, "Of course, but why?"

"Because it's cool." was his response – not because it was the best method of covering information. It clearly wasn't! But to him, being cool was more important than being effective and professional. During his presentation, however, he was neither.

He had missed a basic tenet of communication. The content and the delivery method should be driven by what the audience needs, not be what is convenient (or cool) for the presenter.

Let's take a closer look at the infatuation many presenters have displayed about a few selected evolving hardware options.

Many years ago the technology of choice for corporate training and academic facilities was chalk and the blackboard. They worked well, but eventually a new device – the overhead projector – came on the scene. The blackboard took a back seat. Training facilities and schools proudly announced that every classroom was equipped with a permanent screen and an overhead projector!

Many of those training companies and schools even conducted seminars on how to create and use transparencies effectively, just as we do today with computer based material! It was the high-tech of the day.

In time, though, the overhead projector was replaced by two-by-two-inch slides and remote controlled projectors. Again, numerous training programs provided information and instruction on effective production and use. It was always easy to identify presenters at meetings because they were the ones carrying the materials and hardware "de jour." But soon, the slides, too, disappeared.

The current new technology – the computer – is now the device of choice. It too, is widely used because of its flexibility and contribution to presentations.

But like the previous devices, it will likely be replaced by another new device with which people will "fall in love" – for a while.

In all relationships, both personal and corporate – it's important to use discretion when making a commitment. As businesspeople, teachers, trainers, or communicators, it's important for us to avoid the pitfalls that can come if we "fall in love too easily" with the technology.

The current devices will disappear and be replaced by new "toys." And people will then wonder how they ever got along without those.

Remember to apply sound communication and instructional principles before selecting tools to implement ideas. Use a specific tool because it is the best approach for covering content – not because "It's cool."

Be wary of the lure of infatuation when new and exciting capabilities present themselves in the latest hardware.

Don't fall in love too easily with what might be just a brief encounter.

New Tech But Low Performance

If you put clean water into one end of a garden hose, clean water will come out the other end. But if you put dirty water into one end of that hose, dirty water will come out the other end." This is a picturesque, but sharp, adage that can guide businesspeople who develop and send information about their products and services.

As more communication technology comes on the business scene, we see that garden hose analogy play out – but not necessarily well in the minds of some users.

Here's the problem. As the use of tablets and Smartphone's expands and their capabilities increase, many businesspeople think producing a video segment is a good idea – and easy.

All that is necessary is pointing the camera at a subject, pushing a button, and starting to talk. That will certainly produce a video, but it might also produce a communication disaster at the same time.

Anyone can record a segment of video material, but it takes knowledge to produce a quality product.

Let's look at this from two perspectives – those who work behind the scenes to produce the videos and those who appear on screen.

In the "old days" of movie musicals, Mickey Rooney and Judy Garland could say, "Let's put on a show," when they had an empty barn, eight friends, and a piano. It looked easy, but it wasn't.

When businesspeople today decide to do a video they need knowledge and support to be successful because it takes more than a few words and a location to produce a "simple" message.

It takes "Production." It takes an understanding of the video medium – where to place the camera, where to position the speaker, how to light the location, how to display objects, and how to assure being heard.

It also requires attention to how the people on camera look and sound in order to make the event appear professional.

And it requires consideration of the audience. Today's viewing audience has been exposed to video for all or most of their lives. They are sophisticated viewers who expect quality video and audio. If they don't get that, they turn off the program. It is naive to expect them to view poor quality material!

Here's another adage to keep on mind. "If you make an audience work to understand a message – they won't!"

Corporate personnel responsible for producing video material should focus on these skills when they stream video, schedule a pod cast, a webinar, or a videoconference.

Here's another area where coaching and production are important to the success of video material. Organizations are increasingly using Skype to interview job applicants., and the cost for time and travel is reduced because no one has to go anywhere.

The problem, however, is it places unexpected pressure on the applicant who might have little or no experience with the process. He or she must "perform" well. Certainly not as an actor, but by using skills and techniques that will present a strong and professional image – the image the interviewers will judge. Some of those skills include how to sit or stand, where to look, where to place the tablet or computer, how to describe and emphasize concepts and ideas. What is usually done automatically in face-to-face conversations often doesn't appear on video.

The interviewers have the easy jobs. They just ask questions and then evaluate responses.

There are many instances and stories in business about powerful candidates who don't "come across" well during Skype interviews. If they haven't learned how to appear on video, it is unfair and a disservice to judge them on a video showing. If they have not been appropriately coached and prepared for the experience the interviewers are at fault.

As a corporate decision maker, be sure applicants know how to appear strong and comfortable. If you don't offer that, you just might lose a great candidate because of your own oversight.

And if you are the one to be interviewed, get coaching and advice on how to use the medium. Then practice before the event!

Intrusive Robots

In six of the *Star Wars* films, R2-D2 and C-3PO are important and helpful participants. They are intelligent and curious, and they're polite!

They're helpful, and they respond to other characters rather than intrude on others. In most instances they are welcome additions to groups, and they contribute to conversations.

Too bad the same things can't be said for the robots with which we now come in contact on a daily basis.

I'm not focusing on the robots that build cars and populate other manufacturing facilities. I'm referring to the ones who interrupt our meal times and assure us, among other promises, "I'm not selling anything." or "You've just won an all-expense paid trip to ____." (Fill in the blank)

I'm referring to the "Robocalls," the phone call that usually arrives just when we least want to receive one. Within this category, I'm including both the recorded calls and the calls from real people in call centers whose primary assignment is to make as many calls as possible during their work shift. Of course, by calling at dinnertime they have a greater chance of having someone answer the phone.

But why do company personnel think anyone will buy something from an uninvited stranger? Because robocalls are surprisingly profitable.

I reviewed a computer page on the Internet recently, and on a single screen, the left side revealed methods and reasons to avoid robocalls, but on the right side of the same screen was a list of companies providing assistance in setting up such calls. Just pick your priority.

One company in particular proudly announced it had been active in the business since 1987, and since that time had placed 1.5 billion calls for clients. Do the arithmetic. That works out to approximately two calls every second of every day for more than twenty-seven years.

The company boasted it had helped: "clients make sales," "politicians get elected." "make car, plane, and hotel reservations," and "conduct surveys." It's difficult, however, to fathom why people would purchase products and services from a disembodied voice making an interruptive call at an inconvenient time.

That's counter to most other business presentations where building relationships is of paramount importance. Most successful selling relies on listening to a potential customer to determine what he or she wants.

Robecalls don't listen; they pitch, and they promise.

We interrupt this chapter for a special message.

I just received a robocall in which the "robot" was pitching a special free vacation package for which I would be eligible if only I would agree to "verify" some personal information on this recorded call to assure I was the one the robot thought I was. It was a very short call. I hung up.

The robot would be able to check off one more phone call – but no sale!

Now let's return to our chapter already in progress.

If you ever have the time – and the inclination – here's an amusing way to spend a few minutes with a live "robocaller."

Ask questions about details, specifications, schedules, options, alternatives, and anything else you can conjure up. In a relatively short time, the "robot" will most likely hang up on you!

Time is money and you're wasting the robot's time. But it takes up some of your time, too.

The simple facts related to robocalling seem to reinforce that "Do not call" lists, caller ID indicators, and "incoming" messages on your television screen just don't work. Their intrusion is as much a fact of life today as the short amber traffic light, crowded seats on airplanes, and people sitting next to you talking loudly on their cell phones.

The technology is becoming so intrusive, and we are relying on it so heavily that it might be a productive exercise to re-read or read for the first time – the 1920 play, *RUR (Rossum's Universal Robots)* to see where we might be headed. That play, by the way, is the genesis of the word "Robot."

But, if you do, turn off your phone so your reading isn't interrupted.

Flying Cars and Webinars

Periodically, everyone in business situations is faced with the need to compromise or to agree to trade-offs. Such flexibility shows a need to adapt to change and to take advantage of developments.

But trade-offs and compromise must be applied with caution.

Recently, I was going through a stack of publications that had accumulated over time and which covered a wide range of material, from corporate training to auto mechanics to new technology.

Many people claim they don't believe in coincidences, and they might have a point, but I came across a number of items in that stack that seemed to be related, even though the sources and the disciplines were quite different.

When I read two particularly interesting articles, one from the automobile magazine and the other from the corporate training publication, I was struck by what I saw to be a clear common thread.

Coincidence? I don't know, but I thought the parallels were interesting. Here's what I observed.

The auto mechanics magazine had an extensive piece extolling the capabilities of a flying automobile – the kind of family vehicle George Jetson used in the animated television program.

Although the pilot, Glenn Curtis, patented the first flying car in 1917, the current version is still far from a commercial success. It's an interesting concept, but it remains to be seen if it will ever become a reality.

Here's the trade-off that must be considered and reconciled.

Most likely, the flying car won't have either the high performance of a true automobile or the flight characteristics of a production airplane. It will be able to perform some of the tasks of each type of vehicle, but it won't measure up to the capabilities of either of the originals.

The performance will likely be described as "adequate." That's the nature of compromise where something is given up in order to acquire something else.

Likewise, the article in the corporate training publication described the "trade off" necessary to use "new technology" in place of traditional techniques.

By definition, the traditional instructional environment has limitations imposed by location and time. Just as in the days of Socrates, the instructor and the participants have to be in the same place at the same time.

That system worked well, but technology now has made it possible to move information rather than people, yielding significant and extensive economic benefits. An instructor in one location can converse with multiple participants in countless other places in real-time, and no one has to travel great distances.

Content can be sent, stored, and retrieved from small, easily transportable devices. Much of the material is the same. However, the live, multi-dimensional human interaction is replaced by two-dimensional electronic images. A picture of the person replaces the real person.

The Ohio State University professor, Edgar Dale, described educational participation as ranging from concrete to abstract activities. In what he described as the "Cone of Experience," he showed that the complexity of learning increases as one moves from live, multi-sensory activities to representations of the activity – moving from "doing and feeling" to "showing and telling."

Learning can occur at all the levels, of course, but the degree of abstraction produces different reactions. For example: standing on the rim of the Grand Canyon is a completely different experience from looking at a video or a photograph of the scene.

The same basic information is transferred, but the experience is quite different.

In business situations we're experiencing an accelerating use of technology. Webinars and virtual presentations, for example, are replacing traditional instruction. While the information is similar, like the Grand Canyon example, the impact is different.

Techniques that might work in a classroom don't necessarily transfer to a mediated experience – and vice versa!

Here's the take-away. The flying car and the webinar might be "adequate," but the changing technology might require a change in expectations.

We should embrace change, but we need to learn how to use it effectively and efficiently.

Our goal is to be good – not just "adequate."

A Good Year or a Bad One?

When most of us hear the date 1984, we have an almost instantaneous negative reaction and recall George Orwell's *1984*. His novel certainly presents a lasting picture of frightening social and governmental environments.

Orwell's fictional *1984* is a world to be avoided. But, as with many factors in life, much of the reaction is in "the eye of the beholder." So, here's a different perspective of the year 1984.

In today's real world, 1984 was when Steve Jobs introduced the first Apple Macintosh computer on January twenty-fourth. It featured a nine-inch screen and a price tag of $2,500. It contributed to changing the world, but it didn't even have the capacity of today's Smartphone.

Today it's difficult to think of a world without computers. For the Millennial generation, it's next to impossible. Computers have always existed in their world, and they learned how to use them just as their elders learned to use rotary dial phones, record players, and tape recorders.

Where are those devices now? Gone!

In business, however, we are constantly reminded that, no matter the technology, the requirements are still the same: quality products and services provided to customers in a considerate and expedient manner.

Easy to say – sometimes difficult to do, but essential to master, and necessary to practice constantly.

In *Alice In Wonderland* (one of my favorite resource books), the Red Queen told Alice, "You have to run as fast as you can just to stay in the same place. If you want to get somewhere, you'll have to run at least twice as fast."

What might the business environment look like thirty years from now? Will we be ready for it? No one knows, but consider the trend mathematicians refer to as the "J curve." It describes the increasing rate at which factors change during identical specified time periods.

A simple example: "Pac-man" was a popular and engrossing computer game thirty years ago, but look at the games people, even young children, play today. What might be available in 2044? Probably far beyond 3-D and holograms and into complete immersion and total tactile surround.

But with all these potential changes the person-to-person interactions in business still will be of paramount importance. Customers will expect –and deserve – respect and attention. And they will expect it to be faster than it is today.

Delivery and storage systems will be different, but expectations and consideration will remain.

In order to remain viable and to be successful, businesspeople will have to learn new skills to master effective communication with customers and colleagues. Businesses will be conducted differently, but the motivation will remain the same -to sell products and services.

Academic institutions will likely change, too, in order to help students learn more in less time. Methodologies will change to fit new schedules and curriculum pressures.

And the change won't be simply using tablets rather than chalkboards or whiteboards.

It will likely be as dramatic as when Jerrold Zacharias, Professor of Physics at MIT, founded the Physical Science Study Committee in 1956 and "re-invented" how physics courses were taught in high schools across the country.

Schools themselves will likely change too and no longer consist of age-based groups following specific time schedules in fixed classrooms.

That system worked well in the past, but we're quickly moving into a new world that will demand new approaches to learning, selling, and conducting business.

But all of those changes will still relate to people. Consider this.

Seventy years from now puts us in the year 2084, a century after the Orwell date. But seventy years ago we were just emerging from World War II, and certainly times have changed dramatically since then.

The "toys" are more complex and sophisticated, but people continue to look for the same basics that have always been important.

We can view 1984 as either a frightening world or as the dawn of the exciting and challenging world we now inhabit.

It's all a matter of perspective.

Clever Marketing or Something Else?

With increasing frequency, organizations are restricting access to information and making it difficult for some people to get.

The responsible parties at those organizations don't feel they are discriminating against anyone. They believe they are increasing options and opportunities for their customers by using some of the newer communication tools at their disposal. They believe they are providing expanded services.

To an extent, that's true – for some people. But others are excluded and can't get access to information that is readily available to others. Is that clever marketing, or is it something less positive – like discrimination?

What's the cause, and what's the issue?

Clearly and simply the cause is increased use of available technology.

The very systems and techniques that expand access to information do just the opposite when they are ill-used. Here's what's happening.

Material is printed in newspapers, magazines, newsletters, and a host of other "paper" vehicles – to which there is easy access, but that material often includes comments like, "For more details, go to *www.newspapername.com*," or "To learn about the outcome of the conflict go to *www.magazinetitle.com*."

Access to that additional information is determined by access to a computer. No computer? Sorry. You can't have all that other information. That's limited to the "other" people.

Lack of access to the computer content separates those who can get the additional information from those who can't.

The producers of the material, therefore, decide who gets it. Is that clever marketing, or does it discriminate because access to a computer determines who gets the information?

If an individual chooses not to purchase a computer, that's one thing, but if he or she can't afford it, that's quite another issue. Even those who say computers are available elsewhere – in libraries and other "centers" – assume that people have memberships or transportation capabilities that might not be available to them.

So, their access is related to their income or circumstances.

It's quite possible that some people do elect not to acquire computers

because of cost, or technical competency, or just plain stubbornness. But those are personal choices customers make.

Here's another instance of questionable corporate limitations. With some organizations it's almost impossible to locate a telephone number to talk to a real person.

Web sites usually offer multiple links, but phone numbers are few and far between. Obviously this is a deliberate decision. Organizations are limiting customer access by controlling it to what is convenient for the company.

Customers are forced to play the game the organization selects, but the results of that game are often customer frustration. Good for business?

Even when a caller is motivated and determined to talk to a person, the results are often negative. Here's a case in point. I found the "hidden" phone number of a major company the old-fashioned way. I called the telephone company information number and got the company phone number I needed.

I placed three calls to that number, and after listening to the ever-present menu, I was connected to an extension. That sounded promising, but when the extension was connected I heard a recorded message saying, "I'm sorry I missed your call. I'm either out of the office or on another line. Leave a message, and I'll call you back."

Call number four was even worse because, after hearing the standard message, another, very pleasant recorded, voice informed me, "This mail box is full. Call again later." The call then abruptly disconnected! That time I couldn't even leave a message. How's that for customer service and access to information?

It's worthwhile to review policies and procedures regarding customer access to information because customers deserve access to information.

Using computers or hard-to-locate phone numbers to limit such access are organizational risks. Customers, current or potential, might seek out other communication lines that are open and ready for business. It doesn't make sense to encourage annoyed customers to look in other locations. They just might go elsewhere to do their business.

And they just might find what they want and ignore the options they find difficult to navigate.

CHAPTER 7

Laughable Language

Last week a man handed me an announcement to read at the beginning of a celebration. It began with a four-letter abbreviation, which I didn't recognize. When I asked him about it, he said, "You know that."

I didn't, and when he told me, I said jokingly, "Don't talk in code."

When I thought about that later in the day I realized how often businesspeople talk in code. Look at these abbreviations for example. AMA – NEA. Abbreviations are, indeed, codes because selected letters stand for words and other symbols.

It's interesting to note that codes are usually used to preserve secrecy, but they also serve as time-savers – verbal shorthand.

But the verbal shorthand contribution is effective only when both the sender and the receiver know the "secret code."

Experience can affect what we think coded messages mean. Go back a few sentences. What does that first well-known abbreviation (code) stand for? Does it mean American Medical Association, American Motorcyclist Association, American Management Association, American Marketing Association?

They're all correct, of course, but messages can be clouded by a wrong assumption.

I attended a conference not long ago, and unfortunately, I arrived a few minutes after the keynote speaker began her presentation. She was explaining a specific role for the NEA, and as the talk went on, I became disturbed by her recommendations. I was waiting for the question-answer session to start so I could respond. Fortunately, in her concluding sentence she said, "That's why it's important for the National Endowment for the Arts to take action quickly." Her NEA was not my NEA!

My NEA was the National Education Association, and from my perspective, that NEA had no business being involved with anything she recommended. Her NEA, however, had much to contribute. Understanding the code made all the difference.

Another code we deal with every day is one which most of us take for granted. Language is a complex code, and when we learn the symbols and the conventions, we can communicate in that code.

THE LOWLY TURTLE

Language is like a game in that respect. If we know the rules, we can play the game. Without knowing the rules, there can be chaos. Fortunately for most of us, we simply "grow" into our language. Here's a story that demonstrates how we learn and accept language codes without question.

When I was a school principal, a first-grade teacher told me she was having a problem with one of her pupils. Suzie couldn't read even though she was a very bright little girl.

I asked Suzie's mother to schedule an appointment, and she came in the next day – concerned but argumentative.

The teacher, the mother, Suzie, and I met in a small conference room. Suzie's mother opened the conversation by saying, "I don't know why you're having a problem. We read together all the time."

I said to the mother, "Please show us, because we aren't being successful?'

"Certainly." the mother said. She sat down opposite Suzie and placed a book between them. Mother read the first line and Suzie read the second line – perfectly. Mother read line three. Suzie read line four.

We knew immediately what had happened. Because of the placement of the book, Suzie had learned to read backwards and upside-down!

That sounds incredible, but think about it. When we learn to read, the funny marks on the page are just that – funny marks on the page. They take on meaning as we become familiar with them. Tracking those funny little marks from left to right and from top to bottom are conventions that are part of our code.

Many languages use codes far different from ours, and they all work.

With effort and practice we can master codes other than our own, but we must be careful that our readers know and understand what code we're using.

Encoding a message might be easy for us, but a reader's ability to accurately decode it is essential for effective and productive communication.

From You To We

In many relations – both business and personal – a single word can signal a complete change of position and relationship – if we catch it.

A pronoun can make all the difference.

Here are two instances in which relationships were tense, if not quite hostile, but a complete change in the relationship was illustrated by a simple vocabulary change.

The first one took place many years ago when a young priest, my wife, and I produced a television special for WCBS-TV in Chicago.

We had shot a great deal of footage with the assistance and guidance of a network cameraman. The three of us did a rough edit to select the appropriate footage, and then we were connected with the senior editor to complete the project,

The editor, John, was gracious at our first meeting, but it was clear that being assigned by management to "help" us was not of paramount importance to him. It was certainly not a "résumé enhancer" in his eyes. When all the equipment was ready he said, "What do you want first?"

When we gave him the time code numbers for the opening sequence he typed the appropriate keys on his console and set the first scene. He turned to us and said, "What do you want next?"

We gave him the time code numbers, and he completed the next edit.

This continued for a while, and the four of us were slowly making progress. John continued to ask, "What do you want next?"

And we fed him numbers. With one sentence though, John changed the chemistry in the editing suite when he said, "I think what we could do here is dissolve to the long shot of the garden."

He had suggested the next scene to be added to the story line. It was no longer "you." It had suddenly become "we."

The three of us looked at each other and smiled. John had just signaled he was comfortable working with us. We knew what we were doing.

Because John knew what his equipment could do and what additional footage was in the station's library to support anything we needed, the remainder of the editing session was smooth and productive.

We produced an excellent one-hour documentary that received strong positive evaluations and, ultimately, a "Creative Production" award. With John's full participation, the program was far better than we could have produced alone.

John's switch form "you" to "we" changed the course and the results of the editing process.

The second example of such a "you" to "we" shift happened just a few weeks ago demonstrating the shift is independent of time constraints.

My wife and I were assisting a close relative with some emotionally draining decisions about arranging care for his severely ill wife. As is often the case in such situations, numerous forms had to be filled out and submitted in order to assure the care and availability of a residence.

He was distracted and a bit lost in the process so our support was important.

The administrative clerk in charge of the process was curt and distant. (Say "not very helpful.") Her sentences were filled with, "This is what you have to do." "You need to provide this additional information," "You have to make an appointment to complete this application." "When you have the information, call me." "You – You – You."

He was lost!

When my wife explained the situation, empathy entered the discussion, and she began to help him. Her language and word choices changed to "we." "Here's what we need to do." "We'll get this arranged by next week."

"We'll be able to finish this quickly." "Let's see what else we need."

She became a different person, and the tension disappeared. Everything was handled easily because she knew what had to be done, and she helped him make the necessary decisions without confusion.

Both of these events teach us a lesson as we deal with difficult colleagues and customers.

Avoid the distances and the tensions associated with the word "You."

Replace it with "we."

Relationships will change immediately because collaboration will replace confrontation.

Get It Right

Storytelling is a popular technique in business writing and presentation delivery so here's a very short story related to accuracy in communications. It has three brief sections.

First. Last week I read about a new propulsion system designed specifically for small powerboats. It was fascinating, but my eyes literally popped out of my head when I saw the price.

That's an erroneous sentence!

Second. When I realized what I had just written about the boat and my eyes, I made a 360-degree turn and started over again.

That's an erroneous sentence, too!

Third. As we examine our personal and business behaviors related to speech and writing, it's important for all of us to be deliberate and to walk the walk regarding accuracy in order to avoid misleading or confusing our listeners and readers.

That's another erroneous sentence!

What's wrong with these three sentences? We're exposed to such examples every day, and they seem to be okay. Why did I label them as "erroneous?" Here's why.

Speakers and writers use those words for emphasis or in order to be dramatic; and that's a good thing. But they often choose and use wrong words. Thai's a bad thing.

Here's why the words are wrong. In the first sentence, the word, "literally" was used for emphasis, but the correct meaning of the word indicates a precise description of an event. It means the action actually happened.

But my eyes are still where they belong near the top of my face. They weren't ejected (thankfully) or went rolling around on my desk. "Literally" is simply the wrong word to use, and it behooves all of us to stop using it the wrong way. That includes the professional newsreaders on television and program hosts on radio talk shows, too.

In the second sentence, the intent is to show a dramatic change of course and embarking in a new direction.

But even a quick glance at a compass will show that if you turn 360 degrees from any location you'll be in exactly the same place when you complete the turn.

What people who make such a statement intend to indicate is making a complete reversal in order to set a new course opposite to the current one. They want to make a complete turn and start over again. The correct adjustment would be to make a 180-degree turn. That way the speaker or writer would have made a complete U-turn. That's the intended meaning.

The problem with the third example is it just doesn't communicate what is intended.

The intention is to indicate someone is taking a firm stand on an issue. He or she intends to demonstrate strength and commitment by actually doing something, and not just talking about it.

The intention is good, but the message is confused. The intended message should be designed to show someone taking action – doing something not just talking. The sentence relates to the adage telling us "Talk is cheap. Actions count."

The sentence should be "Walk the Talk." It grew out of debates and demonstrations related to civic conflicts decades ago when many people "talked a good line," but didn't do what they said they would do.

That behavior and that language continue to grow even today.

"Walk the Talk" means doing what you say you'll do. It reflects the adage, "Actions speak louder than words." It mimics my often-quoted first grade teacher who told us, "Say what you mean. And mean what you say."

Even though the erroneous sentences are growing in popularity, using them incorrectly (as many people do) demonstrates a lack of knowledge, and others interpret it as an attempt to appear smart and glib. All it demonstrates, however, is the ability to use hollow words that create little substance.

So, on occasions when you intend to state a position firmly and demonstrate your commitment but find you're being too wordy, make a 180-degree change in course; literally describe your behaviors and your commitment; and then Walk The Talk.

It's easy, and it won't confuse readers and listeners.

Available vs. Accessible

It's interesting to recognize how many of us in various businesses make the same assumptions every day about information we distribute and the customer contacts we design. Many businesspeople have become facile with the "new technology," and, all too often, many assume everyone else has also acquired those necessary skills. Wrong!

We rely heavily on the ever-increasing variety of technologies to process and transmit information about products, services, and alternatives; but some of our intended recipients never receive what we develop.

For many of us, it's hard to believe that there are still some people "out there" who don't use, or even own; a computer. Yet so much of what we transmit to prospective customers is almost exclusively transmitted via the computer and similar related technologies.

That's analogous to sending a semaphore message to a man who is blind. The transmitted message is crystal clear to the signalman, but the intended recipient can't access it because the reception relies on visual acuity.

During the business day we often hear comments like, "I sent you a detailed email yesterday explaining the entire process." That sounds good, but if the response is, "I didn't get an email from you yesterday," whose fault is that? The one sending the message or the one who didn't receive it? Is either one truly at fault?

There may not be a simple answer to that question, but here is something to consider as we ponder it.

Information can't be just *available*; it must be *accessible*.

It isn't sufficient to have it or to send it. That's just the beginning of the communication process. True communication doesn't occur until information is received and interpreted.

Just having the ability to send a message is like using really big flags to send that semaphore signal. It doesn't work!

So, as we conduct our business affairs and send messages about products and services to current and prospective customers we need to begin by asking ourselves some simple questions.

Will my intended audience be able to receive this information? Will they then be able to get at it – to access it? Will they be able to understand the code I'm using? If the answer isn't "Yes" to all of these questions, it's probably a good idea to reconsider our actions.

We don't yet know how to transmit information through mental telepathy so all messages must rely on codes, and knowing the codes is essential to sending and to receiving any message.

A sender can't achieve his intent if the receiving parties can't "break the code." I saw an interesting example of this in a fast food restaurant recently. It read, "Picture menus are available for customers who are unable to read the language." The restaurant operators were thoughtful and sincere in providing the service, but the method created a problem. How could anyone who was unable to read the language understand the information contained in the sign?

For those who don't own, don't want, or don't know how to use the new technologies; computers, lap tops, tablets, and Smartphone provide no useful information. All of those devises contain vast quantities of data, but without knowing how to operate them, they are little more than metal, glass, and plastic. Just like the components of an automobile headlight or a microwave oven.

Once again, it's access, not simply availability that fosters communication.

Techniques and technologies might be exciting to the tech savvy businessperson, but if potential and desired customers can't get at the stored information, the technology offers nothing to them.

I'm reminded of the often-repeated call of the early miners out west as they traveled west when they saw the towering landscapes surrounding them. "There's gold in them thar hills."

They were right. There was plenty of gold, but until someone figured out how to get at it and get it out of the ground, all they had was lots of rocks and dirt.

That wasn't worth very much to them then, and neither is inaccessible information worth anything to anyone now.

The Word's the Thing

Every once in a while it's important to take a close look at the words we use in print. The spoken word is forgiving because the sound is all-important. In print, however, the way a word is spelled determines what it means. As our grammar school teachers often said, "Spelling counts."

In the "good olde days," whenever they were, printed material usually went through two or three stages before it reached a reader. Businesspeople had secretaries who knew how to spell, and publications had layers of editors and proofreaders who corrected and fine-tuned copy.

Today, many of us are our own writers, proofreaders, and editors. That multiple responsibility often results in errors – sometimes funny but sometimes serious.

Here are a couple of recent examples. These two errors recently appeared in newspaper and television news stories. In one story, a sign used at a protest rally read, "We our calling for your help."

The other story showed a poster painted by high school students who were proudly proclaiming their Senior Prom by announcing, "This is are time." The example is serious not only because high school seniors made the poster that included the error, but also because adult faculty advisors didn't catch the error. The students were just days away from graduating, and their teachers missed a chance to avoid a negative image.

Let's take a look at an encounter demonstrating the difference between the spoken word and words in print. I took a few liberties with the dialog because I didn't have a recorder handy, and I had to work from memory. Here's what was said. It sounded fine. but it might be a bit difficult to read.

Too business executives stood at the airline counter wondering ware there plain was. It was scheduled to arrive write at three o'clock, but it was already fore fifteen, and their was know aircraft in site.

Charles, the older won, complained to the gait agent about missing his connection, and threatened to Sioux the airline if the delay caused him to lose a contract he was negotiating.

"Yore going to pay for this. Yule bee hereing from my lawyer before the weak is out."

"I'm sorry, sir, but there is nothing whee can do about the schedule. It's a whether problem wee can't control.

The other man, the shorter won, chimed in. "There's something wrong with my boarding pass. It shows aisle be seated at a window, but I reserved an isle seat. Will you oar a colleague tri to fix that fore me? I can't sit at the window because I'm claustrophobic. You better move me write aweigh."

"Will sea what we mite be able to do after we bored the plain. There could be an empty I'll seat then."

The first man stepped back to the counter and asked, "With the flight being delayed, will their be food service? The last thyme I eight was at noon. Dew you plan to have food on the flight?"

"I called catering. All they said was they'll sea what mite be available. Their are know plans fore a full meal. There will be sum snacks, but don't look fore anything else."

"This airline used to have class, but no more."

"Our knew management seas things differently from your impression, and they our the ones making awl the decisions fore the hole company. We have too dew what they tell us."

A loud speaker announced, "Your plain just landed. Will be boarding inn just a few minutes. Thank you for your patients."

This might seem silly to you. But in business, we are constantly producing and authorizing printed material. We are typing our own email correspondence, and it will live for a long time on the computers and in the minds of our customers. That image and the impact deserve caution and attention because readers often remember mistakes far longer than they remember strengths.

Creating accurate and positive impressions deserves our time and attention, and readers do, too.

What's in a Word?

The English language is filled with words that contain many shades of meaning. Of all the words we have at our disposal, no two mean precisely the same thing. There are similarities, of course, but there are also vast differences. Here's an example.

In describing how something smells, we can choose from, smell, fragrance, aroma, odor, or stench. There are many more, but this selection is sufficient to make the point.

All of the words are about the sense of smell, but they convey vastly different messages – if we recognize the words and know their definitions.

If an expensive perfume or after shave lotion were to be described as having "an unusual stench" sales probably wouldn't be very good. "An interesting fragrance" might be acceptable, but "an intriguing odor" wouldn't.

In business, in government, and in personal life words are our primary tools. We "sell" ideas, products, and services through the words we choose. And we select the words that will have a specific impact on our audiences and customers.

Our words – spoken, in print, or electronic – convey thoughts and messages to others.

As speakers, it's important to be aware of the impact specific words have on listeners, and as listeners, it's equally important to be aware of what a speaker is conveying – really conveying.

The lesson when we sell products, services, or ideas is summed up in this simple sentence, "Words mean things." Be careful and be aware of what sentences are saying – and/or what message someone intends you to conclude.

Language is so flexible that people with broad vocabularies can play "word games" and fool listeners into believing they have heard something that wasn't actually said.

The danger in such situations rests in the fact that listeners usually take a word at its face value. The listener thinks he or she knows what a word means.

An example: We've all heard people make a statement in an interview or a speech, and then later, when confronted with contradictory information, excuse away the original comment by saying, "I misspoke."

What "misspoke" means in such situations is, "I didn't tell the truth" or "I exaggerated a bit," or simply, "I lied, and I got caught."

Selecting the word "misspoke" makes the lie seem insignificant. But it's still a lie, and audiences and customers remember.

Just imagine how a customer feels and would likely respond if a sales person were to quote one price for an item and then charge a higher price. "I misspoke" won't make everything right, and the impression remains.

Remember the poem in which Sir Walter Scott wrote, "Oh, What a tangled web we weave when first we practice to deceive."

Some cleaver speakers and businesspeople get away with deception – for a while – but then reality appears, and confidence disappears. So do the customers and the supporters.

In the long run, it's easier to tell the truth than to "Shade" it, but that often takes strength. A little "white lie" might smooth the day, but it grows, becomes shaded, and relationships suffer. And that "shading" requires a very good memory to be able to recall what was previously said in different circumstances.

Here's where the clarity of the language can be helpful when the "right" word is selected. Usually, difficult decisions become a matter of simply selecting between two options. Yes/No. Stop/Go. Good/Bad. Up/Down. True/False. Legal/Illegal.

In any business or personal interaction anyone avoiding such clear options is seen to be evasive, and evasive translates to untrustworthy or dishonest. On the other hand, if listeners interpret evasiveness as being unsure their conclusion might be the speaker is unprepared or uninformed.

As with all other aspects of effective communication, the words are important, but so is the delivery. For example, how someone says, "No" to a request can be interpreted as harsh or as reluctant. The packaging and delivery of any message are significant, but first, the message itself must be clear.

Fancy wrapping never makes a tasteless gift anything other than tasteless.

So, say what you mean; say it clearly; and mean it.

Preserve and Protect Your Opinions

Not long ago while reading a newspaper I saw something that made no sense. The person who wrote the item was sincere, but the position espoused was foolish. It might even qualify to be called "naive" or even "dangerous." Here it is.

The person wrote an "opinion" letter to the newspaper saying there should be no political, religious, or cultural opinion letters published in the newspaper because opinions are biased.

Think about that for a moment. The writer used the paper to voice an opinion about not including opinions in the paper. But in our society everyone is entitled to have them – and to express them freely.

Readers may agree or disagree, but the opinion is valid even if it is disagreeable.

The fact the author took the newspaper to task and stated the opinion that opinions should not be printed gives one reason to pause.

If opinions are to be censored, the first question is: "Who does the censoring?" Immediately, we can see that the opinion of the official censor is imposed on everyone.

In present day jargon, such opinions might be called regulations or mandates, but they are still opinions.

Just think about what would happen to our businesses if someone's "opinion" were to be imposed on all of us. We would no longer be able to choose what we sell, where we shop, what we eat, where we travel, how we dress, the cars we drive, the fuel we use, and the places we live. Everything and everyone would be the same.

Our ability to make choices makes our lives and our businesses exciting, rewarding, and profitable. When we identify needs and opportunities, we are free to develop and offer unique solutions. Sometimes that's challenging, but challenges are good. They demand responses and individual actions. If a single opinion leader ever became all-powerful, no one could make creative decisions anymore. The "opinion setter" does all the thinking for everyone. The rest of the people simply follow that lead.

On the one hand, that might seem inviting. Imagine having someone else make all your decisions for you. Life would be easy.

On the other hand, that would mean you would have to do what someone else decides is good for you.

For many of us, the cost of such an arrangement would be too high and could destroy our businesses and our life style. In most instances when someone else is deciding what is good for us, it's really good for that other someone.

Conversely, when managers and business leaders solicit and value diverse opinions offered by colleagues and customers, their subsequent decisions benefit everyone.

Varied and diverse opinions related to business services and products fine-tune those decisions and result in stronger operation. One size does not fit all, and one version of the world doesn't represent all possibilities.

Our society, our businesses, and our culture reflect words attributed to various writers, including Voltaire, who is often given credit for saying, "I may disagree with what you say, but I will defend to the death your right to say it."

And that brings me to the final point of this column.

It's always interesting how ideas come together. The "opinion" letter arrived just a week before the anniversary of an important day related to our freedom to make personal choices

Monday, November eleventh, Veterans Day, deserves our attention and acknowledgement.

A statement from the US Department of Veterans Affairs states:

"Veterans Day is intended to thank and honor all those who served honorably in the military – in wartime or peacetime. Veterans Day is intended to thank living veterans for their service, to acknowledge that their contributions to our national security are appreciated, and to underscore the fact that all those who served – not only those who died – have sacrificed and done their duty."

So consider a couple of suggestions: Fly the flag. Thank a vet. And remember the dangerous restrictions suggested by that letter writer.

Let your opinion be heard – and respect the value of the opinions you hear.

More Words, Words, Words

Recently, I wrote about common errors in word usage, and many readers identified additional errors. Here is a sample of those suggestions and reminders about correct usage.

Before we begin, here's a caveat. In this day and age, political correctness dictates using both masculine and feminine pronouns at all times to demonstrate inclusion. However, to make this material flow smoothly I'll use the "old way" and stay with the masculine, even though both genders are included.

So here we go. Do you use "bring" or "take;" "who" or "whom;" "that" or "who;" "less" or "fewer;" "in" or "into"? Let's look at our options and point out distinctions. They're all easy to remember if we use care, but old habits die hard for most of us, so little thought will help. Here we go.

The words "bring" and "take" describe direction. That's all we have to remember.

"Bring" indicates moving *toward* the speaker/writer. "Take" indicates moving *away* from him. Example: "Bring two copies of the report to my office for signature, and take your copy when you leave." Here's another. "After you take the car this evening, I expect you to bring it back with a full tank of gas."

Those two sentences describe both the action and the direction.

"Who" and "whom" are often confused, but it's easy to remember the correct usage. "Who" is the actor or the doer in a sentence. "Whom" is the receiver. Here's a simple example. In a library or classroom, you might hear this question. "Who gave the book to whom?" The relationship is easy to understand even though it sounds a bit like the old Abbott and Costello "Who's On First" comedy routine. (Younger readers might have to search for that on Google.)

We see the next error every day in supermarkets where the express checkout lanes are designated by signs that clearly state, "Ten Items or Less." Brief, but wrong.

"Less" indicates amount. "Fewer" designates number. Examples: "The trip will take less time, because this revised route requires making fewer stops." Here's another. "Charlie purchased less gasoline because he drove fewer miles."

When you can count individual items, use "fewer." When there is a designated quantity, use "less."

Another common error results from confusing people with things. That should be easy to avoid because the item in question either breathes or it doesn't. Consider the difference between "that" and "who." Obviously, "that" is a thing, and "who" is a person.

Example: The author who attended the seminar wrote the book that you bought.

For most of us it's easy to tell the difference between a person and a thing, so all we have to do is think about what we're saying. Most people won't argue about the benefits of thinking before speaking.

This final example of word usage is something we hear and see often in newspapers, on radio and television, and in daily conversation. The images such misuse conjures up can be funny when you visualize them. This is the misuse of "in" and "into."

"In" denotes a specific place, but "into" indicates movement from one place to another. Example. The milk is in the refrigerator. I'll carry the other packages into the kitchen." The first is a place; the second is movement.

Why can misuse be funny? Consider the difference between jumping "in" the water and jumping "into" the water. If you plan to jump in the water, you must be wet already, but if you plan to jump into the water you're still on a rock, a dock, or a dive platform. They're little words, but they convey vast differences.

You'll make it easier for your listener or reader to understand what you mean when you select the correct word.

We've said this before. "We're judged by the words we use." So, in every business situation be sure to use the right ones."

CHAPTER 8

Message Clarity

Messages we want to send are very clear as we think about them, but to get them to someone else requires caution and care.

We don't know how to send thought messages yet so we have to use codes – spoken words, visuals, in print, on line, or through gestures.

Like sending Morse code or Semaphore, we have to know the code, and the rules for using the codes.

Misuse can lead us to "misspeak" when we use symbols in correctly where "Yes" can become "No"; "Up" becomes "Down"; or a host of other errors.

Once sent though those errors cannot be returned or "unsent."

What Was The Actual Message?

Often, it's difficult to determine if some people who write copy for TV, radio, newspapers, or corporate PR are "clueless" – or think their readers and listeners are gullible – or not very smart.

Such confusing and deceptive copy doesn't just "happen all by itself." Someone has to take the time to develop the ideas, write the words, and distribute them through selected channels. Whenever such material is produced, writers have a specific audience in mind.

And it seems some of those writers must have low opinions of their readers and viewers. The words they select and the messages they conjure up are designed to mislead – to fool – perhaps even to lie, and they get away with it.

When readers don't – or can't – take the time to dissect such messages, they are deceived. Here's an example I found recently.

A commercial for an automobile insurance company offers a clever statement that describes how in a claim payment made after an accident the owner of a new $35,000 car will not receive the full amount needed to replace his car. The company will pay only $33,000 even though the owner had the car for just 3 weeks.

The announcer proudly proclaims his company will "pay the full value of the car." Sounds great, but "full value" isn't "replacement cost." The value of a car is quite different – less than what it would cost to replace the car. The insurance company commercial sounds good, but it is misleading. Intentional?

Here's another example. A finance company catering to a specific patriotic segment advertises that, "Because of your past service, we guarantee you will qualify to apply for a one hundred percent loan for the value of your house."

Again, that sounds better than what other lending companies offer, but the claim actually guarantees only that the customer can apply for the loan – not that he or she will actually get it, and anybody can apply for a loan. Intentionally misleading?

And, we've all been tempted by advertising that promises "Up to…" some amount that might be intriguing. Maybe we even fell for the temptation. But when something is promised as amounting "up to…" it means it could also be much less! Intentional or accidental?

Here's another example. Amusement parks and even some other types of institutions attract customers by using advertising copy that promises, "All rides are free." But further on additional text adds, "with paid admission." Huh? Intentional?

Like many others listed on a purchased mailing list, I recently received a promotional piece from an automobile dealership announcing I was "guaranteed" to win one of four designated prizes ranging from a new car to a golden coin. All I had to do was visit the dealership with an attached fake key and see if my scratch-off numbers matched the numbers at the dealership.

The hook here, of course, was the guarantee of winning at least a golden coin. A moment of thought resulted in seeing the difference between a "golden" coin and a "gold" coin. Intentional deception?

I'm sure we could easily document many additional examples of questionable copy like these examples. Such "creative writing" may not be intentionally dishonest, but it can certainly be misleading. It is designed to attract customers. And it works!

Rather than taking such messages at face value, look at them as intellectual exercises. We would do well to ask ourselves this question. "Do I see and hear what is being offered, or am I seeing and hearing what I want to see and hear?" It's easy to jump to conclusions when we think we're receiving what seems to be good news.

The old adage, "Caveat emptor," "Let the buyer beware," is still excellent advice.

We all have many opportunities to participate in these commercial word games but just remember this other piece of advice, "Words mean things."

Be aware of the goals of all the parties, know what the words really say, and be sure of the possible misunderstandings, accidental or deliberate, at all times.

Know the rules of the word games, and follow them at all times.

Who Writes This Stuff?

Here's something often forgotten. Companies don't

write letters – people do. When mail arrives under an impressive letterhead, we often respond to the perceived power of the stationery. But, let's explore examples of a few of those letters.

Letters often are written to customers in order to evoke – or provoke – a reply. But sometimes it's difficult to determine the real purpose of the document.

Here are three examples of actual letters to customers. These letters demonstrate a lack of concern for maintaining relationships even though most businesses rely on preserving and strengthening relationships with customers.

The first example was sent by a bank executive to a customer who had only one payment left on his home mortgage. Quite an accomplishment – one to be recognized and worthy of a compliment.

It's reasonable to expect such a letter would say something like, "Thank you for being a good customer for so long. If you ever need our financial assistance again please let us know so we can be of service to you once more."

But this letter said, "Your final payment is due in thirty days from the above date. Please remit via cashier's check. A personal check will not be accepted. If your payment is not received by the noted date, it will be necessary to turn your account over to a collection agency in order to conclude our relationship.

"Please be prompt with your final payment so that this action will not be necessary."

One wonders what business school – or one-day seminar – he attended!

Someone in a major retail store sent this second letter to a long-time customer. It said, "You have not used your credit card in a considerable period of time. If you do not use your card within the next thirty days, your account will be closed, and the card will no longer be valid."

There was no thank-you for being a customer, no request for information about why such a long-time customer was no longer using the card, nothing asking what could be done to retain the customer. The message was just a straight forward, "Use it or lose it."

And, by the way, that recipient had maintained the account since 1962. That could likely be longer than the letter writer had been walking this earth. He or she might have attended the same business school as the banker.

The final example has an interesting touch of humor – dark humor. An accounting department associate, thinking he could enhance his status in his company, composed a letter he sent to all customers who had bills outstanding for more than thirty days.

Without clearing the text with his supervisor, this associate wrote, "If your account is not settled within thirty days from the date of this notice, we will turn over your account to our lawyers."

He assumed such a threat would get quick action and prompt payment – and a commendation from his management.

One such threatening "Payment Due" letter went to a very large corporation that promptly replied. Handwritten in the margin of his original dunning letter was a simple response from that company (no check included). It said, "Our lawyers are bigger than your lawyers."

A noted copy was sent to the president of the billing company.

Needless to say, the unilateral action by the well-intentioned associate did not result in the reputation and the praise he expected.

We don't know what business school he attended either, but his communication skills needed a lot of work.

The takeaway for all of us from these three examples is this: Be sure your letters really say what you mean them to say. What will they say to the people who receive them? Don't create more problems than you're solving.

When writing a potentially controversial letter, leave it in a desk drawer overnight. Read it again in the morning. And, finally, have someone else read the letter to be sure it sends the right message with the appropriate tone.

Any questions?

Typos Tell Many Tales
(Or is it "Tails"?)

Typos give me a headache. I have a feeling there is some "force" lurking in the atmosphere – or cyberspace – that constantly forms them at will – like the "Gremlins" of World War II fame.

It seems that no matter how many times a text is reviewed, edited, and revised, typos continue to appear.

When a book I wrote was published recently, a friend found some typos. And he was quick to tell me about them. During editing, I hadn't seen them, nor did the two editors who worked on the book spot them. Somehow they just seemed to show up. That's impossible, of course. Someone typed the erroneous material. It wasn't intentional, but that final version with the typos continues to exist. Sometimes the eyes don't see what they're looking at.

I suspect my friend won't remember everything included in what I wrote, but he'll remember the typos, and he'll probably mention them to others, too.

It's impossible to explain or justify why typos are so commonplace now. I'm currently reading a book by a well-known, very successful author, and it too contains numerous typos.

What has happened to accuracy?

In the "days of yesteryear" the structure and the execution of books and newspapers stood as models for accurate writing. That doesn't seem to be the case anymore.

I'm not suggesting a cause-effect relationship exists here, but there seems to be a correlation between expanded use of electronic technology and accuracy in writing.

Users of the new electronic technology – with email and texting – seem to have placed a higher priority on speed than on accuracy. The abbreviations of the "texting language" have replaced words, and in some cases, entire sentences.

Those "messages" don't require the precision of using traditional writing conventions, but in business it's important to realize these changes have become a new and different language.

They should not, however, be allowed to replace the old language.

In fact, technological developments require we all become multi-lingual.

The writing skills and techniques that are appropriate for one segment of the business community should not overpower the skills and techniques appropriate for other segments of the population.

It would be beneficial and productive if all of us learned new languages well enough to manage the changing readership.

An adage related to writing effectiveness says, "To be a good writer, you must become your reader."

In some instances, that reader might be more interested in the speed than in the techniques. In other situations the precision of the execution of the language skills might be more significant.

When there are multiple levels and preferences within the reading audience, it's important to select and aim for the appropriate relationship.

All readers and writers want clear messages, and I'm not aware of any segments of the various categories that promote intentional errors.

So it seems to be in everyone's best interest to be precise. Typos denote carelessness, and when the appearance of a message illustrates a lack of precision, the content also is called into question. Not good.

If a writer is perceived to be careless and unconcerned with accuracy because of typos, readers may not grasp the importance of the content. Creating and encouraging disinterest in the mind of the reader risks becoming a self-fulfilling prophecy. When readers observe errors in print, that image lasts. Therefore, it's in our own best interest to strive for and to request accuracy in all the written material we offer to customers. What we provide speaks volumes about us, and it's important that those volumes contain only accurate and positive messages.

Most readers don't separate the work of the writer from the work of the editor. In their minds, if there is a typo, it reflects poorly on the writer – not the editor. That's the way the world operates.

We all know its poor business to deliver a poor quality product, so it just makes sense for everyone concerned to portray nothing but a first class image.

Blueprints or Handcuffs?

In many business situations, I've heard recurring concerns about presentations and reports in which presenters must use the approved corporate template. That template defines and restricts all the elements of a talk including the font size, the font style, the colors, the layout, and the sequence.

The intention behind requiring templates, of course, is a positive one, but often the result is "cookie-cutter" presentations. The structure of the template determines how the content will be disclosed rather than the content determining how the presentation will look.

It's the reverse of the adage, "Form Follows Function." Being required to use corporate template becomes, "Function Follows Form."

If that credo were to be applied to other situations, every car, for example, would look like every other car, and every piece of clothing would look like every other piece of clothing. There are similarities, of course, but in the automotive world and the clothing world the differences determine the design. Those differences are the result of performance and appearance expectations, not simply following the dictates of a corporate template or one-size-fits-all blueprint.

I have observed businesspeople struggling with their material in order to make it "fit" the requirements of a template. That's simply the wrong emphasis because presenters are forced to fit the square peg into the round hole. Something has to be cut off or cut out in order to get the peg into the hole.

There is another unnecessary restriction resulting from requiring presenters to use templates. Presentations are built backward. Deciding *how* material is presented should be the last step – not the first one in the process. Depending upon the audience, intentions, locations, data, expectations, and a host of other variables, the delivery techniques will vary, resulting in using computers, or handouts, or flipcharts, or tablets, or maybe even a chalkboard!

It's important to pick the right tool for the job.

A colleague delivered a presentation at an academic institution a while ago, and he was told to use their template. Also, he was told to send the talk to the conference organizers in advance of the conference. All presentations would be included on a DVD every attendee would receive.

He declined to send his material because he planned to use handouts and a flipchart in order to cover his material appropriately. An interesting tug-of-war ensued between him and the organizers. Up until the day before the conference, the organizers insisted on the computer version.

For his presentation, he used handouts and a flipchart.

I sat through the thirteen presentations as they were presented at the conference, and they all looked the same. It's difficult to remember the content covered in one from the others. His presentation, however, stood out because the material drove the delivery – not the other way around. The feedback he received from the audience affirmed the value of his decision.

Generally speaking, it seems presenters fall into the trap of being hardware driven. Years ago the presenter identification symbol at any meeting was the carousel projector tray filled with two-by-two-inch slides.

Today, although the technology has changed, the dependence on hardware seems to remain.

So here's an alternative way to plan and execute a presentation. First, determine what you want to convey. Next, get a good grasp of the specific characteristics of your audience. Then, identify what you want them to learn from your presentation. Finally, decide the best way to communicate your message.

There can be one additional problem with templates. Their structure often results in using an overabundance of words because templates assume the presentation can stand alone.

In a presentation, visuals should support, not replace or restrict a presenter so be sure to let the message define the techniques – not the other way around.

Of course, common sense must prevail. If your company absolutely requires you to use a template, use it if you intend to remain on the payroll,. But if you have any flexibility these alternatives will help.

Avoidable Errors

Recently, I read a promotional piece on the importance of appearance in business. The points were solid, and the advice was valuable, but there was a significant problem.

The piece contained two grammatical errors. Singular and plural subjects didn't match their predicates.

The printed word, on paper or on a computer screen, speaks volumes about the writer. I found it interesting the writer didn't place the same level of significance on using correct language as he did to wearing "proper" clothing.

In this age of political correctness, I want to point out I used the masculine, "he," because the writer is a man. I don't want to be faulted with an error in a chapter about errors.

There is a developing movement to eliminate gender words and replace "he" and "she" with "ze." I have no idea if that will ever catch on, but remember how "Miss" and "Mrs." became "Ms." I used "he" to be precise, and there is much to be said in favor of gender accuracy rather than "gender correctness."

In yet another business communication – this time an invitation to a gala event at a resort – the very first sentence contained a serious error.

The invitation opened with this line, "It's not *to* late…" Even elementary school grammar lessons clearly indicate the word, "to" is a preposition. The correct word in the invitation should have been "too." "It's not too late…"

Is grammatical accuracy really necessary? In the minds of some, the answer to that question might be, "No." Printed text, however, lives on long after the spoken word, and the repeated message it delivers defines both the writer and the organization he or she represents.

Image is important, and regardless of how we may feel about grammatical accuracy, many in the business world value it, and they judge others by what they learned to be "right" or "wrong" when they were in school.

In many instances people excuse their errors by stating, "You know what I mean. What's the big deal?"

More and more, we're communicating in abbreviations as text messaging increases. The language of texting requires using an entirely new language. That's fine, but it's important to avoid mixing multiple languages in a single vehicle.

Texting requires mastering abbreviations that can be understood only in context. For example, AAF can mean "Always and forever," or it can mean, "As a friend." LOL can mean "Lots of love" or "Laugh out loud."

Very different, and context is essential for understanding. There's nothing wrong with texting, but it requires learning a separate language with its own set of rules.

Now here's a question. If someone takes the time and exerts the effort to learn the text language, why not take the time and exert the effort to master the rules of the standard language, too?

The most appropriate answer, I suppose, is a matter on motivation. Many people simply "want" to learn the text language. It's part of their everyday lives. The standard language, however, draws a "Why bother?" response. "What difference does it make? No one cares about that anymore."

The simple truth, however, is that many people do care, and many of them are in positions to evaluate us and to affect our careers.

Language usage has an impact on audiences – formal or informal.

We all use different languages during the course of the workday, and the most productive strategy is to match the language to the audience.

Effective communication is always about what's important to the audience, not just what is comfortable to the speaker or to the writer.

The image we present to our various audiences is significant, and it will last for a long time. No one can be sure where our print or electronic copy will surface in the future, so it's in our own best interest to be careful about what we send.

None of us will ever achieve perfection. Even though that's beyond our grasp, however, it's a good idea to work toward it and to avoid the avoidable.

Thank You

Have you ever noticed how difficult it is for most people to accept a compliment by simply saying, "Thank you"?

They qualify the response with some kind of additional comment. When you stop to think about it, that qualification diminishes the intent of the compliment. It actually says to the person offering the compliment, "There's something you don't know" or "You're not as perceptive as you think you are."

That's insulting!

Here are a couple of examples I've heard over the years.

After an excellent vocal performance, a fan said to the singer, "That was beautiful." The singer then responded, "Thank you, but I hit a couple of bad notes right at the end."

Here's another. Arriving at a dinner party, a guest told the host, "I saw your new car in the driveway. It's beautiful." The host's response was, "Thanks. It isn't the color I wanted, but it's nice. "

A woman, complimented by a friend about a new dress said, "Oh, this old thing. Thank you. It's been in the back of my closet for the past year."

You can probably add more from your own experiences, but in every one of these examples the interchange would have been better, friendlier, more sincere if the receiver just said, "Thank you," and stopped taking.

A compliment is a gift from one person to another. By downplaying or diminishing it, the receiver rejects or minimizes that gift.

Because a compliment is given freely, without qualification, it should be accepted freely – without qualification.

In that first example about a singer, the fan didn't say, "Except for those last couple of bad notes, that was beautiful." Just imagine how the singer would have reacted to that!

The interesting part of this kind of interaction is the simple fact that no one is required to extend a compliment – about a performance, or a car, or a dress. It's given freely, and it should be received that way.

On the other hand, there are others who have difficulty extending a compliment so they say nothing. That silence speaks volumes.

When you feel the urge – for any reason – to compliment someone about something, do it, and do it right way.

Often people will say things like, "I wanted to say something, but I just couldn't find the tight words." Here are those "right words." Just fill in the blank spaces with the specific word (sang, looked, spoke, danced, performed, dressed, etc., etc.) and (great, well, beautifully, excited, enthusiastic, informed, etc., etc.)

"You _____ _____ this afternoon."

That's all there is to it. Look the person right in the eye, and speak up.

Such simple sentences have a great impact, and they create a wonderful impression.

If you feel compelled to add any specifics after that first sentence, feel free. It will just add to the impact and to the sincerity. But, even without the additional words, you have already paid the compliment.

If a handshake, a pat on the back, or a hug would be appropriate, add that to your words. It makes a nice package.

Now, here's a "homework assignment."

Seek out opportunities at work, at home, at club meetings, or at parties; and compliment someone about something. Don't make it a major production, just say something about a new tie, the color of a blouse, the delivery of a business presentation, or anything else; and then listen for the reaction.

Is it, "Thank you, but"? Is it, "Thank you, and…"? Is it "Thank you. I got it from ___." Or is it simply "Thank you."

Chances are you'll hear the exception more frequently than the simple, "Thank you."

Try it out this week, and see what happens.

Finally, when the time changed last Spring I gave incorrect advice about the direction of the change, and I received many letters about the error. So remember Daylight Saving Time ends on November 6, 2016. Turn your clocks BACK one hour before you go to bed on November 5, 2016.

You'll thank me in the morning. And I'll say, "You're welcome."

CHAPTER 9

Generational Differences

Much has been printed and said about the conflicts associated with interactions of Traditionals, Baby Boomers, Generation Xs, and Generation Ys.

It's important not to think of the four groups as adversaries. They simply look at and evaluate situations from different perspectives and different experiences.

All of them make decisions on the basis of their observations, and the differences are similar to the story of "the blind men and the elephant." Each of the men acquired information by touch, and because each one touched a different part of the elephant, their interpretations were different.

None of them was more or less accurate in his perception – just different.

The multi-generational work force is just like that. All of us perceive events and situations by our own experiences and limitations.

Open exchanges of ideas and perceptions will result in clearer perception by all parties.

That's beneficial for everyone.

New Normal

No business, no product, no workers are the same today as they were months or years ago. Everything changes. Nothing stays the same.

An interesting term entered our vocabularies a few years ago, and its use is exploding exponentially to the point the Australian newspaper, "The Australian," gave it a term, "cliché of the week."

Of course clichés come and go as language continues to change, but this new term – The New Normal – seems to describe declining standards or reduced expectations

It's interesting to speculate why the words "The New Normal" have been closely associated with reduction rather than improvement.

In the business world, the words are associated with lower salaries, poorer customer service, and fewer jobs. In academia they justify lower test scores and performance, and in the workforce they justify longer completion times, and increasingly poor quality outcomes.

In short, the term seems to be related to and be a justification for lower performance standards.

It's almost impossible to identify anything wherein a "new normal" is an improvement over the "old normal." It seems to be an excuse for poor performance. It's shirking responsibility. It's giving up and accepting what shouldn't be acceptable.

It's giving permission and credibility for something that should be eliminated – or at least – improved.

In short, calling something the new normal is surrendering. It's the latest version of "It is what it is."

I've not seen or heard any reference to "the new normal" as something to be desired. It's never an improvement! In old street jargon, "It's a cop out."

Unfortunately, we have become conditioned to accept the words themselves rather than exploring and confirming the meaning of the words, and we justify the conclusions. As soon as we hear the words, "new normal" we're quick to accept the new condition. It's like being happy when we learn that our temperature or blood pressure is "normal" The reaction is "All is good. Life is good. Nothing to worry about."

Although the term "New Normal" first appeared in 2009 and focused on economic factors and jobless rates, it has now expanded into multiple facets of our daily lives where we are lulled into accepting mediocrity rather than working for improvement – for excellence.

Mediocrity is easy. Just lower expectations, and you'll never be disappointed.

Chicago baseball fans used to say that about the Cubs at the beginning of every season when debating prospects for the outcome of the season.

The major problem with such a dialogue is that if it is spoken long enough people begin to accept it as truth.

Most people believe that the way things are now is the way they will always be. Not so! And the way they are now is not what they were in the past.

That reflects the message of the first paragraph. Everything changes. The determining factor is the role we play in the changes. If we blithely accept the "New Normal" that's exactly what we'll get.

The big question is, "Is that what we want?" It's a matter of choice, and choices are everywhere.

During the past three weeks there have been important historical observances, but in most cases those observations were accompanied with little or no celebrations.

First there was Memorial Day with lots of product sales. Then there was D-Day, but it too was met with little recognition. Tomorrow is Flag Day, and so far there is little indication there will be any acknowledgement.

Not too long ago all three of those dates were observed by displaying the American flag. Today it's difficult to find the flag anywhere. Businesses, schools, and offices once proudly flew the flag. Today very few people even note the reasons for the events.

Perhaps the "New Normal" is forgetting the significant events in our history. That would be sad, so here's a suggestion.

Let's establish a new 'New Normal." Make it positive. Let's recognize our gifts and our responsibilities.

In the opening paragraph we acknowledged that things change. With some specific choices, it will be possible to create that change and once again recognize and honor our history.

What's Down The Pike?

In one hundred years – all new people."

That was inscribed on a plaque a friend kept on his desk. And the inscription was on both sides of the plaque so he and visitors could read it.

Quite understandably, many people didn't like it – because it made them uncomfortable. However, he believed it was a thought-provoking sentence that was useful for business planning, both long term and short term.

He held to the concept he learned from the American Management Association that stated, "Long range planning isn't about making future decisions, but rather about the future implications of current decisions."

He saw the constantly changing populations as an important factor in planning and operating any business. Many in business seem to concentrate on "what worked" in the past, and they overlook the fact that the past is gone. What's coming should determine current actions.

But even that perception can send distracting signals, and result in inappropriate activities and possibilities.

Here's an interesting case in point. Today's business environment places great emphasis on the "new" technology, and that technology certainly has had a hand in current business operations because they aren't static.

There are constantly new tools, new challenges, new options, and of course new people to operate them. Concentrating on what worked in the past is analogous to driving a car while looking in the rear view mirror. It's important to know what's behind you, but as an old outdated TV commercial said, "It's what's up front that counts."

It's easy and tempting to become enamored with the new devices, but remember that classroom tools once included stereopticons, wire recorders, and flash cards. Professional business offices, likewise, were equipped with ditto copiers and mimeograph machines. (Some readers might not even recognize those terms now.)

It's easy to forget how quickly some tools and technologies become old and outdated.

I was reminded of that on a recent trip to Chicago when I read an article in a local newspaper detailing the demise of Saturday morning television cartoons on all three major network stations., although they're still on many cable stations.

The writer was contemplating his father-to-be reaction years from now when he would have to take away his children's tablets when it was time for bed, and he concluded the article by saying, "If there's even such a thing as a tablet by then."

It's difficult to imagine a world without tablets and Smartphone's, but it will happen, and they'll be replaced by a future generation of new technology for use by the eventual "all new people."

Rather than thinking of my friend's plaque as something uncomfortable, I think of it as a challenge and an opportunity to ask such questions as, "What will we then have at our disposal?" "What will we be able to do with it?" "How can we help people to use and learn with it?"

Now, all this new technology and all those new people won't appear suddenly, of course. They will evolve, and if we watch carefully, we'll be able to see the trends; and evolve with them. If we don't look for those changes we might find ourselves reaching for the equivalent of the latest version of Pac Man or a 78-RPM vinyl record of a favorite song.

Bob Dylan told us in his song that, "The Times They Are A-Changin'."

Be ready and greet the changes so businesses will remain viable and successful. We don't know what's ahead, but we can embrace the changes and be inspired and challenged by them.

Put aside the pessimistic and fatalistic adage, "It is what it is." Rather, ask what we can do about "it" and how we can get ready for "it."

In the musical *West Side Story*, Steven Sondheim presented all of us with a wonderful perspective as well as a beautiful song lyric when, in collaboration with Leonard Bernstein, he wrote, "Something's coming. I don't know what it is, but it is gonna be great."

Maybe Find Another Way?

A number of years ago I learned a lesson unexpectedly. And it spoke of the old adage, "If you become a teacher, you'll learn from your students." That's precisely what happened one day as I was teaching a seminar on business writing to a group of very successful salespeople.

In fact, this group of eleven represented the very top salespeople in a major US corporation. They included both male and female and a wide age range. Further, I was probably the youngest person in the room.

One of the participants, the most senior of the group, Chris, was just three and a half weeks from retirement. But here he was – in the class.

Given the group's make up, I felt a bit intimidated. I always opened such programs saying, "Although we'll be covering some material that might be familiar, this is not a remedial education program. We'll be adding to what you already know, and we'll be offering new options you'll be able to incorporate in your business assignments."

We started out well. Participation and attention were good Then the "Yeah, but…" comments began. Many participants didn't agree with or see the value of some of the suggestions being made.

I was losing ground – and credibility – quickly. But suddenly everything changed! Chris spoke up from the rear of the room. "Hold on. Let's listen to what he has to say. He could be offering us some good new material. We just might learn something important."

It was clear everyone respected his opinion. They all stopped the, "Yeah, but…" and the comments became much more positive and conversational. Chris had changed the course of the program – for which I was appreciative.

But the lesson I learned from him that morning resonated with me on the spot and remains until this day.

His behavior also demonstrated why he was the top salesman in the company.

Although he was leaving the company in only a few weeks, he was still interested in "learning something." He could have sat there in the rear of the room watching the time tick past, but he didn't. He stayed fully engaged in the discussion.

Through his actions, as well as numerous comments he made during the day, it was clear he seized opportunities that came his way – and had consistently done that in business and in his private life.

He told me during a break he had other things that needed his attention, but as long as he had to be in this classroom. "I might as well learn whatever I can."

That was a strong example of how he practiced "self-talk," the technique we described recently that can have a profound impact on all of us.

He chose to be involved that day when he could have easily "tuned out" and simply put in time. His behavior, however, demonstrated how and why he had become so successful in his career.

He had been fully involved in the past and, based on his comments, he planned to continue to be involved in multiple activities after retirement – a little more than three weeks away.

Chris' story is profound and a powerful lesson for all of us as we move through our own careers and our personal development. He summed up his philosophy in these two words, "Keep learning."

As technology changes, as processes expand, as each of us faces challenges and opportunities, we can't rely solely on what we already know. We can't depend on the comment. "I know what I like, and I like what I know." If we reject or resist change, the world will pass us by.

It's easy to see how typewriters and carbon paper have been replaced by computers and printers. In time those devices, too. will be replaced by other devises as yet unknown.

Just speculate for a moment on what our business environment might be like in just a decade from now.

Be ready. Stay ready by following Chris' example. Embrace opportunities.

Remember: change is inevitable, but growth is optional.

CHAPTER 10

Just For Fun

Sometimes it's productive just to have a good time – to enjoy opportunities.
These essays are for that purpose.
Enjoy!

Oh, The Words We Select!

The pressures of the political season are increasing, and we're hearing substantial rhetoric from many directions. I thought about some of the common words in presenter's speeches, and I noticed how certain words show up in everyday use, too.

Without actually counting, one of the most frequently used words is: "Fight."

Everyone is promising to "fight" for something. Sounds strong and tough, but I'll bet most of them haven't had a real fight since a lunchbox dispute during recess in the first grade.

I have no idea if that's true, of course, but I hope the exaggeration makes a point. They won't fight; they'll "work," but that doesn't sound very powerful.

"Fight" is a word intended to deceive in political speeches, but we must be aware of deception in business dealings, too. We're not elected to serve multiple-year terms. We can lose our "business terms" overnight.

"Fees" is another deceptive word that shows up in many segments of our daily lives. Don't be fooled. Here are some examples.

Airlines now charge baggage fees, a fee for a better seat, and a fee for rescheduling a reservation. They don't increase prices because that wouldn't look good. "Fees," however, can be added and manipulated at will.

Even closer to home than air travel are the "fees" parents must pay to provide items and services that should be provided by public school budgets.

Because school boards and administrations operate beyond what is provided by taxes, they add "fees" for all kinds of things including lab fees, book fees, art fees, supply fees, athletic fees, and extra-curricular fees, to name only a few.

Such "fees" are simply tax increases without benefit of discussion or the chance to vote.

Speakers in the public spotlight have taken to using – incorrectly – another word in order to sound firm and passionate. That word is "literally." It sounds strong, but it creates erroneous messages. The word means something is a statement of fact. It is an exact description without exaggeration. But if someone says, "My eyes literally popped out of my head." that's just plain foolish. And gruesome.

The correct word there, of course, would be "figuratively," but it doesn't sound as strong, and people sometimes sacrifice accuracy for impression.

Here's another interesting word: "Irregardless." It's interesting because it isn't a real word. It sounds "intelligent," though, and is often used by the same people who say "between you and I…" It sounds smart to them, but don't use it!

With increasing frequency, the word, "Look" is used to build a verbal platform before making a statement. It's nothing more than a jumpstart. Often within the sentence that follows "look" we'll hear yet another word: "Fundamental."

It seems our language is now filled with "fundamental changes," "fundamental principles," and "fundamental issues."

Once again it's a matter of image over accuracy, and it becomes redundant and annoying very quickly.

Many other words are misused either because of carelessness or because we never learned the right ones. Here is a brief sample of words that are singular or plural. As a reminder, the first word in each pair is the singular one. Medium – media; criterion – criteria; memorandum – memoranda; datum – data.

Pay attention, and every day you'll hear many of the plural words used when the singular would be correct.

Our language has thousands of words, and no two words mean exactly the same thing. We use only a few of them, but be careful of your choices.

Our words speak volumes about us either in speech or in print. People judge us by the words we use, and even though we might feel that's unfair, it's in our best interest to select the words with care.

In summary, here's a parting thought.

Look. It's up to you and I to literally fight hard to preserve our fundamental language conventions so they remain clear and precise irregardless of changing social pressures.

Okay?

Looking vs. Seeing

A few years ago, a friend painted a word picture that is as clear today as it was then. With a bit of whimsy he described an event we all experience at this time of the year.

"As Autumn begins," he said, "you know Fall has arrived up North because the leaves change color. Here in the South you can tell Fall has arrived because the license plates change color."

Visual signals are powerful, and they have an important impact on us. In fact, visual information probably sends the strongest of all messages.

We take most visual data for granted because we've seen the images so often. When we see what we expect to see, we feel comfortable and assured. Contradictory images, however, are unsettling. Here are some examples:

When we see a commercial airline pilot walking through a major airport terminal we always see a crisp white short-sleeved shirt, polished shoes, a tie, and dark pants. He or she "looks the part," and we feel comfortable.

Think of how you would react if that pilot was dressed in stained shorts, a torn T-shirt, and running shoes. Our comfort level would change if we saw such a person being in charge of the plane we were about to board.

We might even question the advisability of flying with him or her. Even without knowing anything about the person, the credentials, the experience, or the abilities we probably would make a quick judgment.

We all like to believe we are without bias, but we aren't. On a regular basis, we "judge a book by its cover." We categorize people, and we often respond to the very categories we create.

We jump to conclusions about visual images. Often we're right, but we can't assume we're right all the time. That could lead to incorrect and unintended consequences.

The problem is this. We LOOK at many things, but we often don't SEE them. In everyday activity, "looking" can be described as the physical ability to perceive visual images, but "seeing" is the mental and intellectual ability to convert those images into ideas and concepts.

And, how we convert and interpret those visual images is the result of experience. Our frame of reference and our backgrounds influence the conclusions we reach. As experiences increase, so do the number of possible interpretations we might make.

Limited experience leads to simple and simplistic, black-white conclusions. Expanded experience provides us with multiple options. All too often, in interpreting images we find ourselves deferring to the simplistic options because they are fast.

Here's a little self-test I've used in seminars. For the next dozen strangers you see, guess what kind of people they are and what kind of work they do. Decide if you would like to meet them and spend time with them. Then ask yourself, "Why'? or "Why not?"

You probably won't actually meet them, of course, but this experience might present a few lessons about stereotypes, misconceptions, and the accuracy of observations.

And that could be a beneficial lesson for all of us.

Business Decisions Often Come First

Last Sunday, November 6, 2016, Daylight Saving Time ended and won't return until March 12, 2017. For the next four months, we'll have to learn to endure darkness at five p.m. but welcome the light again at six a.m.

Since time was in the news this week and affects all of us, I thought I'd revisit something I discovered a few years ago about time and how it is designated across the country.

We often hear references to doing business twenty-four/seven. The Internet has made that possible, but we must be aware of local times when connecting with clients. My guess is that most business people give little, if any, thought to the genesis of Time Zones.

A logical assumption is that the Federal government developed the concept. However, like many other logical assumptions, that one is incorrect.

The four time zones in the US came from business – specifically the US Railroad industry. As is often the case, the Federal government followed a business decision in adopting the Time Zone designations.

Business days begin and end at approximately the same local times, but because the country includes four time zones, when we plan to make contact with clients and customers it's necessary for us to check not only a clock but also a map. It's easy to find the correct local time in the US because of the clear designation of the boundaries of the time zones, but it wasn't always that way!

I learned about the business contribution years ago when I was walking in downtown Chicago. On the corner of LaSalle and Jackson, I discovered a plaque that describes how the US time zones came into existence. The following text is inscribed on that plaque.

Standard Time System in the United States was adopted on this site on October 11, 1883.

Chicago's famous Grand Pacific Hotel, then on the site of the present Continental Bank building was the location of the General Time Zone Convention of 1883, which, on October eleventh of that year, adopted the current Standard Time System in the United States.

The Convention was called by the nation's railroads. Delegates were asked to develop a better and more uniform time system to govern railroad operations. Previously, time had been determined by the position of the sun with high noon the only existing standard of exact local time.

More than one hundred different local times resulted from this method. The new plan proposed by William F. Allen, convention secretary, established four equal time zones across the country. Each one hour ahead of the zone to its west.

All railroad clocks in each zone were to be synchronized to strike the hour simultaneously. The Standard Time System was inaugurated on November 18, 1883. On that day, known as the "Day of Two Noons," the Allegheny observatory at the University of Pennsylvania transmitted a telegraph signal when it was exactly noon on the 90th meridian. Railroad clocks throughout the US were then reset on the hour according to the time zone.

Although implemented by the railroads; the Federal government, states, and cities began to use the system almost immediately. On March 19, 1918, Congress formally acknowledged the plan by passing the Standard Time Act.

This plaque is presented to the Continental Bank by the Midwest Historical Society, Inc. on November 18, 1971.

Not only was this a significant historical fact, but it also demonstrated another valuable contribution a group of businessmen made to the country.

Thirty-five years passed before Congress formalized the decision the railroad executives made at that meeting.

The Time Zone designation made at the Convention was good for the railroad business, but it was also good for the country.

We've all seen those time zone lines zig zagging down our maps. Now we know who put them there.

If you have the time and the inclination, look at the plaques you pass on your travels.

But don't just look at them; read them. You might discover something interesting.

Remember the Future As Well As the Past

Memorial Day Weekend, is a high-powered business weekend.

It's difficult to pick up a newspaper, watch television, or listen to the radio without being overpowered with advertising. It is a wonderful holiday. We all look forward to it, but I think it deserves a bit of thought that is often overlooked.

Memorial Day is recognition of people who have died to preserve our way of life. In a real sense, Memorial Day is a funeral service. Many people feel strange saying "Happy Memorial Day."

I don't intend this to be morbid, but it is important to recognize the history of the Day. That recognition includes honoring the traditions and the ceremonies that mark the day.

Recently, I saw two photos of men and women in military uniforms saluting the American flag. This is always a moving moment, and as we get closer to Memorial Day we'll probably see many more such photos. Those pictures seemed to be a good idea at first glance, but upon further review, I realized the flag was displayed backward! The blue field was in the top right corner. That's wrong.

There are very specific rules about how the flag should be displayed just as there are rules about displaying a corporate logo. There is a right way and many wrong ways.

Whenever the flag is displayed on a wall, the blue field with the stars is placed at the top left corner. Period. No exceptions. If it is on a pole extending from a wall, the blue field is away from the wall. Remembering just those two rules will take care of most display situations.

Correct flag etiquette is easy to find on the Internet in case you want a reminder when you put up your flag this weekend.

Proper display is a matter of respect, and with a little thought that respect will be evident. With improper display the lack of respect will also be evident.

Memorial Day deserves such respect not only because it's a holiday, but also because it honors all those who died to make all our holidays possible. We have such holidays because people – our ancestors – earned them for us.

And here's something to think about on this holiday. If we don't honor and protect those observances, one day they could be gone. Unfortunately, if that day were to come, many people would express surprise and ask, "What happened?"

And the answer would be "It' happened because we let it happen."

Now, let's change our perspective. Rather than continuing to focus on the past and what others have done for us, for business, society, and family let's look ahead and consider what we might be able to offer to others still to come.

I was struck by the power of a single sentence I recently read, and I think it can provide inspiration and direction for many of us. Just consider this sentence.

"Be a good ancestor."

Let that thought roll around in your head for a while.

What does it mean for us? What can we do with that idea? What impact can it have on us?

When we look at events like those leading up to Memorial Day, it's clear we can't change any of them. We can benefit from them and learn from then, but we can't alter them.

What we can control is what is to come. So here are a few things to consider as we enjoy our Memorial Day celebrations. What are we doing today that will have an impact on the lives of our children, grandchildren, and great-grandchildren? That impact might be positive or negative, but either way we'll be responsible for it.

How are we directing out business activities, and what will our business and our world look like two or three generations from now?

When those future generations look for us on their family tree, what will they find? Will we be pleased and proud of what we did, or will we wish we had done something different?

If that's the case, do the groundwork now so you will indeed "BE A GOOD ANCESTOR."

About the Author

Bob Parkinson has served as a communications consultant and coach for numerous Fortune 500 companies working successfully at all levels of corporate, government, and academic institutions from CEOs to new hires. In addition, he has taught more than 1750 communication related programs for clients in the US and internationally and consulted and conducted research in South America, Africa, and Australia.

He earned a PhD degree from Syracuse University. His other degrees are: MA in Management and Supervision, and BA in English and Biology from Montclair State University (NJ).

After serving on active duty in the US Army, Parkinson began his professional career as a high school teacher. Subsequent professional positions include: Faculty, Northwestern University; Associate Dean, National Louis University; Director of Research, Office of the Governor, IL; Director of Research, Bell & Howell. He lives with his wife, Eileen, in Sarasota, Florida.

www.ingramcontent.com/pod-product-compliance
Lightning Source LLC
Chambersburg PA
CBHW061636040426
42446CB00010B/1446